HUMAN ORIGINS

Tracing Humanity's Evolution

These and other books are included in the
Encyclopedia of Discovery and Invention series:

HUMAN ORIGINS
Tracing Humanity's Evolution

by LOIS WARBURTON

The ENCYCLOPEDIA of
D·I·S·C·O·V·E·R·Y
and INVENTION

P.O. Box 289011 SAN DIEGO, CA 92198-9011

To Amanda Leigh Duquette
evolution's finest product

Library of Congress Cataloging-in-Publication Data

Warburton, Lois, 1938--
    Human origins: tracing humanity's evolution / by Lois
    Warburton.

        p. cm.—(The Encyclopedia of discovery and invention)
    Includes bibliographical references and index.
    Summary: Traces past and present theories of human
    origins and evolution and discusses fossil discoveries and
    their significance.
    ISBN 1-56006-221-5 (acid-free paper)
    1. Man—Origin—Juvenile literature.   2. Human
    evolution—Juvenile literature [1.Man—Origin.   2. Evolution]
    I. Title.   II. Series.
    GN 281.W35 1992
    573.2—dc20   92-24990
                                                            CIP
                                                            AC

Contents

Foreword

The belief in progress has been one of the dominant forces in Western Civilization from the Scientific Revolution of the seventeenth century to the present. Embodied in the idea of progress is the conviction that each generation will be better off than the one that preceded it. Eventually, all peoples will benefit from and share in this better world. R.R. Palmer, in his *History of the Modern World*, calls this belief in progress "a kind of nonreligious faith that the conditions of human life" will continually improve as time goes on.

For over a thousand years prior to the seventeenth century, science had progressed little. Inquiry was largely discouraged, and experimentation, almost nonexistent. As a result, science became regressive and discovery was ignored. Benjamin Farrington, a historian of science, characterized it this way: "Science had failed to become a real force in the life of society. Instead there had arisen a conception of science as a cycle of liberal studies for a privileged minority. Science ceased to be a means of transforming the conditions of life." In short, had this intellectual climate continued, humanity's future would have been little more than a clone of its past.

Fortunately, these circumstances were not destined to last. By the seventeenth and eighteenth centuries, Western society was undergoing radical and favorable changes. And the changes that occurred gave rise to the notion that progress was a real force urging civilization forward. Surpluses of consumer goods were replacing substandard living conditions in most of Western Europe. Rigid class systems were giving way to social mobility. In nations like France and the United States, the lofty principles of democracy and popular sovereignty were being painted in broad, gilded strokes over the fading canvasses of monarchy and despotism.

But more significant than these social, economic, and political changes, the new age witnessed a rebirth of science. Centuries of scientific stagnation began crumbling before a spirit of scientific inquiry that spawned undreamed of technological advances. And it was the discoveries and inventions of scores of men and women that fueled these new technologies, dramatically increasing the ability of humankind to control nature—and, many believed, eventually to guide it.

It is a truism of science and technology that the results derived from observation and experimentation are not finalities. They are part of a process. Each discovery is but one piece in a continuum bridging past and present and heralding an extraordinary future. The heroic age of the Scientific Revolution was simply a start. It laid a foundation upon which succeeding generations of imaginative thinkers could build. It kindled the belief that progress is possible as long as there were gifted men and women who would respond to society's needs. When Antonie van Leeuwenhoek observed *Animalcules* (little animals) through his high-powered microscope in 1683, the discovery did not end there. Others followed who would call these "little animals" bacteria and, in time, recognize their role in the process of health and disease. Robert Koch, a German bacteriologist and winner of the Nobel Prize in Physiology and Medicine, was one of these men. Koch firmly established that bacteria are responsible for causing infectious diseases. He identified, among others, the causative organisms of anthrax and tuberculosis. Alexander Fleming, another Nobel Laureate, progressed still further in the quest to understand and control bacteria. In 1928, Fleming discovered penicillin, the antibiotic wonder drug. Penicillin, and the generations of antibiotics that succeeded it, have done more to prevent premature death than any other discovery in the history of humankind. And as civilization hastens toward the twenty-first century, most agree that the conquest of van Leeuwenhoek's "little animals" will continue.

The *Encyclopedia of Discovery and Invention* examines those discoveries and inventions that have had a sweeping impact on life and thought in the modern world. Each book explores the ideas that led to the invention or discovery, and, more importantly, how the world changed and continues to change because of it. The series also highlights the people behind the achievements—the unique men and women whose singular genius and rich imagination have altered the lives of everyone. Enhanced by photographs and clearly explained technical drawings, these books are comprehensive examinations of the building blocks of human progress.

HUMAN ORIGINS

Tracing Humanity's Evolution

HUMAN ORIGINS

Introduction

The mystery of human origins is one of the most difficult puzzles humans have ever tried to solve. The sheer size of the puzzle is overwhelming, as the mystery spans several continents and thousands of years. It has literally billions of pieces, for every extinct human ancestor and relative from the ancient past is a piece of the puzzle.

So far, out of the billions of human ancestors and relatives who once lived, only a few whole skeletons have been found. Most knowledge has been gleaned from thousands of scattered fossil fragments. Scientists, for example, often speculate on human ancestry with only a jawbone, the back of a skull, or a foot to guide them. Even these pieces of ancient bone are often small, distorted, and worn.

Because of these impediments critics argue that the search for human origins will be fruitless. Human origins, they say, lie buried too deeply in the past for any clear picture to emerge in the present.

Why then do people continue to search for the truth about their origins? What is so intriguing about this age-old mystery? The answer lies in human nature. Humans are the only creatures on

▪▪▪ TIMELINE: HUMAN ORIGINS

> 1   2   3

1 ▪ 1655
Isaac de la Peyrérè publishes a book describing what he believes are stone tools crafted by primitive humans.

2 ▪ 1735
Carolus Linnaeus publishes *Systema Naturae*, cataloging all living things.

3 ▪ 1809
Lamarck publishes his theory that humans slowly evolved from four-footed animals.

4 ▪ 1830
Geologists prove earth is millions of years old.

5 ▪ 1856
Neandertal Man is discovered in Germany.

6 ▪ 1859
Charles Darwin publishes *Origin of Species*.

7 ▪ 1867
German scientist Ernst Haeckel publishes an ancestral tree which reveals his belief that humans evolved from apes.

8 ▪ 1891
Eugene Dubois discovers Java man in Indonesia.

9 ▪ 1912
Piltdown man is discovered in England.

10 ▪ 1924
Australopithecus africanus is discovered in South Africa.

11 ▪ 1926
Peking man is named in China.

12 ▪ 1953
Piltdown man is found to be a fraud.

earth who have self-awareness. They not only know things, but can analyze and interpret what they know. As German psychologist Eric Fromm said:

> Man has intelligence, like other animals . . . but Man has another mental quality which the animal lacks. He is aware of himself, of his past and of his future, which is death; of his smallness and powerlessness; he is aware of others as others—as friends, enemies, or as strangers. Man transcends all other life because he is, for the first time, life aware of itself.

This self-awareness has moved humans to seek out more about the past. By understanding the past—why some ancient ancestors thrived and others went extinct, for example—many people believe humanity will be better prepared to proceed into the future. If, as most scientists believe, evolution is a continuing process, then human beings today represent only the latest stage along a very long, slow path. It is the belief that we cannot discover why we are here and where we are going until we discover where we have been that keeps scientists piecing together the grand puzzle of human origins.

5 > 6 > 7 > 8 > 9 > 10 > 11 > 12 > 13 > 14 > 15 > 16 > 17 > 18 > 19 > 20 > 21 >

13 ■ 1959
Louis and Mary Leakey discover *Australopithecus boisei* in Olduvai Gorge.

14 ■ 1960
Jonathon Leakey discovers *Homo habilis* in Olduvai Gorge. Potassium-argon dating is invented.

15 ■ 1964
Louis Leakey tells the world about the discovery of *Homo habilis*.

16 ■ 1974
Donald Johanson discovers *Australopithecus afarensis* in Ethiopia.

17 ■ 1978
Mary Leakey discovers Laetoli footprints.

18 ■ 1984
Turkana boy, the oldest and most complete *Homo erectus* skeleton ever found, is discovered near Lake Turkana.

19 ■ 1987
Biologists announce African Eve is oldest common ancestor.

20 ■ 1992
Milford Wolpoff announces new evidence supporting the theory that Neandertal man is an ancestor of modern Europeans.

21 ■ 1992
Chinese and American researchers announce they have uncovered evidence indicating that modern humans evolved at the same time in both Africa and Asia.

Early Explanations

Many thousands of years ago, our ancestors began pondering a mystery so big that it still has not been solved. In fact, it may never be completely solved. What they wanted to know is how human life on earth began. Modern scientists, with all their knowledge and resources, have not been able to answer this question, so it is not difficult to imagine how perplexing it must have seemed to prehistoric people. Yet they did come up with some answers.

Many ancient peoples believed that several powerful gods were responsible for creating human beings. But by the fifth century B.C., scholars and others had turned to the mysterious forces of nature and the growing belief in one supreme God for explanations of human origins.

The influential Greek philosopher Plato, for example, believed that every living creature has a set position and purpose in nature and that these do not change or evolve. According to Plato, humans had been created as superior beings and were placed at the top of what he called the great chain of being. Animals had their place much lower down on the chain.

The Biblical Creation

Before long, however, many civilizations had developed another explanation of human origins. This explanation was found in the Bible. According to the Bible, God created the earth and heavens and, at the same time, created humans. He formed man from dust and created the first woman from a man's rib.

Many religious leaders of the day accepted this account as the sole explanation of human origins. Those who openly questioned this explanation were branded as heretics and outcasts. Yet some people, including those with a strong belief in God, did question the

An engraving depicting Adam and Eve. God, the Bible says, created Adam from the dust of the earth and Eve from Adam's rib.

biblical account and wonder if it should be taken as a literal explanation of human origins. Often, they studied other possible explanations in secret.

Anatomical Studies

Italian artist Leonardo da Vinci, for example, decided to investigate other theories. Da Vinci was a genius whose talents spanned the fields of painting, sculpture, engineering, architecture, physics, and philosophy. He had a particularly strong interest in human anatomy. To learn more about anatomy, da Vinci dissected the bodies of apes, monkeys, and humans. He learned a great deal from these studies, which he began in 1493. Much of his work was done in secret, however, because human dissection was forbidden by powerful religious leaders, especially in the Roman Catholic church.

The notes da Vinci kept during these secret studies show that the similarities among humans, apes, and monkeys did not escape his attention. In his notes, he wrote, "Man in fact differs from animals only in his specific [characteristics]."

Da Vinci's discoveries, along with findings by later anatomists, proved that physically, at least, humans are part of the animal world. But this knowledge did not affect most people's thinking about human origins for many years. Throughout the sixteenth, seventeenth, and eighteenth centuries, most people believed that humans were special creatures at the top of the chain of being and were unrelated to any animal species.

Their unwillingness to acknowledge the links between humans and animals was equaled by their refusal to consider

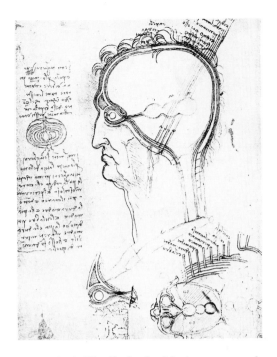

Leonardo da Vinci's sketch of the human central nervous system. His anatomical studies revealed the similarities between human and animal bodies.

the possibility that humans have ancient beginnings and are much older than the Bible suggests. In 1650, an Irish biblical scholar, Archbishop James Ussher, announced that his studies had revealed the year of creation to be 4004 B.C. This strengthened the belief that humanity's origins were relatively recent.

Seventeenth-Century Science

At the same time, however, a few amateur scientists were making some discoveries that caused them to doubt Ussher's date. Frenchman Isaac de la Peyrérè was one of them. He roamed the French countryside collecting an assortment of odd, chipped stones. After examining them carefully, he decided

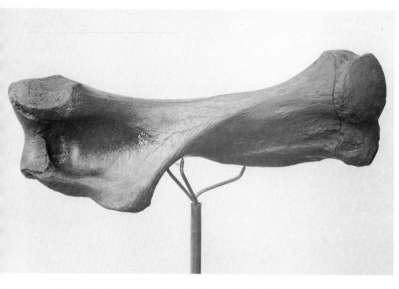

Seventeenth-century scientists thought that fossils like the mastodon bone (left) belonged to an extinct race of monstrous, giant humans. Scientists refused to believe, however, that artifacts like this flint spearhead (right) could have been made by ancient humans because they did not believe humans were ancient beings.

the chips could not have been caused by natural forces. De la Peyrérè believed the stones were actually tools shaped by primitive people and that these people had lived before 4004 B.C. He published his findings in 1655. They met with immediate disapproval, and his book was burned in public.

Humiliations like this stopped most amateur scientists from making similar claims, but it did not kill their curiosity. Quietly, they continued to dig in the dirt and explore caves, and the mysterious stones kept turning up. To add to the mystery, some of these amateur scientists began to uncover giant bones in their digs. These bones were judged to be ancient because they were worn and very brittle. Actually, they were fossils, the preserved bones of extinct animals, such as mammoths and saber-toothed tigers, but no one knew that at the time. Because seventeenth-century people believed in giants and monsters,

they decided these bones had belonged to an old race of giant humans.

The activities of these amateur scientists, who were out scrambling over rocks, digging in gravel pits, and exploring deep into caves to find ancient bones, marked the birth of the science of paleontology, the study of fossils. But by attributing the fossils to giant humans, seventeenth-century paleontologists failed to contribute any knowledge about human origins.

Eighteenth-Century Science

The eighteenth century, on the other hand, was an age of innovation and belief in free thinking, a time when many new ideas appeared. One of these ideas came from Swedish scientist Carolus Linnaeus. Linnaeus believed God had designed nature according to a meaningful, unchanging order. He felt he understood this order. So he designed a system that would allow other scientists to see it, too.

Linnaeus painstakingly classified and named every different kind of plant and animal in a consistent manner. This was important, since new types were constantly being discovered, and until Linnaeus provided a system, there had been no general agreement on how to assign names or determine relationships to other plants or animals.

Linnaeus Classifies Living Things

In 1735, Linnaeus published a pamphlet entitled *Systema Naturae* that cataloged living things according to what he believed was God's design. Although it has been enlarged and changed many times, this system is still being used today and is known as the Linnaean binomial system of nomenclature. *Nomenclature* comes from a Latin word meaning "list of names." *Binomial* means "two names" in Latin, and in this system, every living thing is given two Latin names. The first name designates its genus, a group of organisms that are closely related. Each genus, in turn, is composed of smaller groups that are different from each other. These smaller groups within each genus are known as species. Only organisms of the same species are capable of interbreeding and producing offspring. Linnaeus classified modern people as *Homo sapiens. Homo,* meaning "human," is the genus name. *Sapiens,* meaning "wise," is the species name.

It is clear that Linnaeus recognized the close physical relationship between

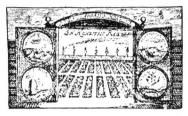

The title page from Carolus Linnaeus's 1735 pamphlet Systema Naturae in which he classified living things. Linnaeus's classification system firmly linked humans and apes.

humans and apes because he said, "I find it most difficult to discover one [characteristic] by which man can be distinguished from apes, unless perhaps in the matter of his [canine teeth]." In fact, Linnaeus actually classified apes with humans by including them in the genus *Homo.* By this time, most scientists were aware there was a link between apes and humans, but no one knew what it was.

Linnaeus was also clear about his beliefs concerning fossils. Since he thought the world was unchanging, he

In the eighteenth century, Swedish scientist Carolus Linnaeus discerned a certain order to creation. He created a system of cataloging species that revealed that order.

believed that fossils could never have been living things. He classified them as stones. But many scientists did not agree. In fact, some paleontologists were beginning to find fossils that anatomists were identifying as human bones, and they were of normal size, not giant. But few scientists were willing to risk their reputations by saying the fossils had belonged to ancient humans. The bones were usually reburied or ignored or explained away.

This was the most practical course because their age could not be proved, and few people believed the earth was old enough to yield ancient human bones anyway. Most people viewed these fossils as nothing more than old bones.

Not until the early nineteenth century did anyone again seriously raise the possibility that humans were the result of a very long, slow, and ancient process. This task was taken on by Jean-

Baptiste Pierre Antoine de Monet, Chevalier de Lamarck. Lamarck, as he was known, had dabbled in many fields. But he devoted himself to developing the theories of his onetime teacher, scientist Georges-Louis Leclerc, Comte de Buffon. In his world history called *Histoire naturelle*, Buffon had declared that everything in nature develops and changes slowly and continuously.

Lamarck added that this process included humans. In *Philosophie zoologique*, published in 1809, Lamarck argued that humans had slowly evolved from four-footed animals to animals that walk on two feet.

Few people supported Lamarck's theory. They preferred to believe a more traditional theory put forth by a contemporary of his, French paleontologist Georges Cuvier. Cuvier stated that humans were a recent creation and that they sat unchanging, alone, and special

In 1809, French naturalist Lamarck theorized that humans evolved from four-footed animals, but few of his contemporaries agreed.

FOSSILS

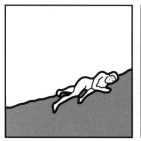 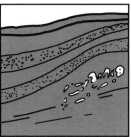 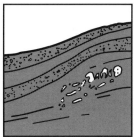 

Fossils are the remains of plants and animals preserved in rock. In animals, usually only the hard parts of the body—the teeth and bones—become fossilized. This happens over thousands of years and only when conditions are just right. First, the body must be buried quickly, for example, under ash from a volcanic explosion or mud from a flood. After burial, the body must lie undisturbed for a very long time. Even then, a bone will not become a fossil unless the soil's moisture and chemical content are right.

The transformation from bone to fossil begins when collagen, or protein, leaves the bones and is replaced by minerals from the ground. The minerals turn the bones to stone, making them hard, heavy, and strong. The soil under which the bones are buried also hardens into rock. Under the pressure of layers of rock, the fossils often break into many tiny fragments.

Then, conditions change. The rock begins to split or erode until finally the layer of rock containing the fossil becomes exposed. Eventually, further erosion washes the fossils out of the rock, and they lie exposed on the surface. This is the moment they must be found, before they are trampled by animals or buried in the mud again.

at the top of the chain of being. He often said: "Human fossils do not exist." Because Cuvier was considered the world's leading paleontologist, no one seriously questioned his version of human origins for another fifty years.

However, Cuvier and most scientists did not question the great age of fossils of other forms of life. The evidence for this came from the new science of geology. During this time, geologists gained new knowledge about the rocks that form the surface of the earth. They discovered that rocks had been formed by the compression of many layers of different types of hardened deposits, one on top of the other. Some of the layers were very thick. The geologists reasoned that it must have taken a long time for so many layers to form. By 1830, there was general agreement among scientists that the earth was not thousands of years old as some believed but many millions of years old.

Ancient Fossils

If the earth were so ancient, then the fossils found in the bottom layers of rocks probably were also ancient. Unfortunately, there was still no scientific way to date the layers, so geologists had no way of knowing how old each deposit was. But they could give the fossils relative dates. A fossil found in one layer had to be older than a fossil found in the layer above it. And it had to be younger than a fossil found in the layer beneath it. It also had to be basically the same age as the other fossils found in the same layer. Various forms of relative dating were the only methods of fossil dating available for many decades.

In fact, at this time, few exact scientific methods of any kind existed. The absence of precise scientific procedures made it even easier to ignore or reject unpopular theories. Despite this, new theories about the earth had set the stage for a revolution in the way most people thought about human origins. That revolution began in 1859, largely because of two ideas.

William Pengelly's careful research persuaded many of his colleagues that humans have lived on earth for millennia.

Prehistoric Humans

The first idea was the notion that humans had actually existed in prehistoric times. Several scientists hastened acceptance of this idea, but perhaps the most influential was Englishman William Pengelly. By the 1850s, most scientists believed those oddly shaped stones amateurs had been collecting for years were really human tools, but no one had yet been able to prove they were ancient. Pengelly set himself the task of finding out whether the tools found in caves beside the fossils of extinct animals were the same age as those fossils. And he approached his task as scientifically as nineteenth-century methods would allow.

First, he looked for a cave that appeared not to have been disturbed for thousands of years. He found it on Windmill Hill above the harbor in Brix-

ham, England. He felt sure the cave had not been disturbed because the stalagmites, or mineral growths, on its floor were large, hard, and even. Stalagmites take thousands of years to grow as the calcium in water that drips from the ceiling forms deposits on the cave floor. A human touch can disrupt this growth. The maturity of the stalagmites told Pengelly the cave had been largely untouched. He took five expert geologists with him so they could not only contribute their expertise but also be witnesses to the fact he had done everything correctly.

Just below the layer of stalagmites, Pengelly found fossils from extinct mammoths, woolly rhinoceroses, cave lions, and cave bears. There, intermingled with the fossils, were stone tools made by humans. Pengelly's discovery convinced many scientists that humans could indeed have been on earth for a very long time. In 1859, England's scientific societies finally agreed that Cuvier had been wrong. Those fossils that anatomists had said looked human could have come from ancient humans after all.

Darwin's Theory of Evolution

The second revolutionary idea introduced in 1859 was Englishman Charles Darwin's theory of evolution. The idea of evolution itself was not new. Lamarck and other scientists had introduced it many years before. By the 1850s, most people had accepted the general notion of evolution, which is the gradual development of life from simple to more complex forms. But Darwin's theory was different. He based his theory on years of extensive research using careful scientific methods, and he offered a scientific explanation of how evolution occurred.

In the 1850s, however, the idea of evolution was acceptable only if it did not include humans. This was part of the reason Darwin kept postponing the announcement of his theory. By 1858, he had already spent twenty-five years seeking scientific proof of his theory. Although Darwin had no direct evidence, he was convinced that evolution applied to humans as well as plants and animals. But he was an extremely cautious man who cared a great deal about what people thought of him. To avoid the uproar he knew his theory would cause, he did not publish his findings and simply continued collecting evidence.

Then, in June 1858, Darwin received a letter and manuscript from British scientist Alfred Russel Wallace.

Wallace had written his own theory of evolution and sought Darwin's comments. Darwin was shocked to see the similarity between Wallace's theory and his own. In order to receive credit for all his years of work, Darwin would have to publish his theory first. Hastily, he wrote a book called *On the Origin of Species by Means of Natural Selection; or, The Preservation of Favoured Races in the Struggle for Life.* When it appeared in the bookstores on November 24, 1859, all 1,250 copies of the first printing sold out in one day. The uproar began immediately, mainly because of one sentence.

Although the book explained evolution almost exclusively in terms of plants and animals, Darwin had decided at least to mention human origins once. In the conclusion, he wrote, "Light will be

Charles Darwin's theory of evolution caused a public uproar because it implied that humans had evolved from lower species, namely, apes.

Famed cartoonist Thomas Nast mocks Darwin's theory in this 1871 cartoon. The ape complains to Henry Bergh (center), the founder of the Society for the Prevention of Cruelty to Animals, that Darwin (right) wants to steal the ape's heritage.

thrown on the origin of man and his history." It was enough. Because his book said all species on earth had evolved from other, similar species, everyone knew what he was implying. According to Darwin, humans had evolved from apes.

The public was outraged. Reactions ranged from the ridicule of newspaper cartoons depicting well-dressed apes to a much-quoted remark by the wife of the bishop of Worcester. When she heard about Darwin's statement, she said to her husband, "My dear, let us hope that it is not true, but if it is, let us pray that it will not become generally known."

The only people who were happy about Darwin's theory were scientists who now had a scientific theory of human origins to investigate. They knew the best way to do that would be to examine human fossils to see how they had evolved, or changed, over great periods of time. It was very frustrating that none of those old bones that had been found were still available. But, in fact, parts of a mysterious, fossilized human skeleton were available for examination. It had been found in 1856, three years before Darwin's book appeared.

CHAPTER 2

Finding the First Fossil

The human fossils found in 1856 were the first to be acknowledged as undeniably human. And so for the first time, scientists had an opportunity to gain new knowledge about human origins by examining concrete evidence from the past. For five years after the fossils were found, however, they contributed no knowledge about human origins. One reason for this was that the deposits that held the fossils had been destroyed, making it impossible to prove their age.

A Discovery in Germany

These bones were found in Germany, in the deep, narrow Neander Valley, a short distance from the city of Dusseldorf. The steep sides of the valley were pitted with caves, and in 1856, some of those caves were being quarried for lime. One day, workmen blasted their way into a cave called Feldhofer Grotto. As they cut through the rubble looking for lime, they discovered some worn, old-looking bones.

The workers showed the bones to one of the quarry owners. He suspected they were fossils from an extinct cave bear and instructed the workers to bring him any bones they uncovered. As it turned out, they found only a few more. The quarry owner took those fossils—the top of the skull or skullcap, some ribs, part of a pelvis, and some limb bones—to a local math teacher and amateur scientist named Johann

Carl Fuhlrott. Fuhlrott had two questions before him. How old were these bones and to what sort of creature had they belonged?

"A Very Ancient Individual"

Fuhlrott had no scientific method for judging the age of the fossils since none had yet been invented. So, he relied mainly on their dark, worn, brittle appearance to determine their age. He decided the bones were ancient.

With his first question answered, Fuhlrott moved on to the next. He examined the bones more closely. Everything he knew about anatomy told him these were human bones, but they were unlike any human bones he had ever seen. The skullcap seemed big enough to have held a human brain, which, Fuhlrott knew from his studies, is larger than an ape's brain. But the walls of the skullcap were unusually thick, and its shape was longer and narrower than a typical human skullcap. In addition, the forehead was low and sloping, much like the forehead of an ape. Strangest of all, the skullcap had massive, bony browridges jutting out above the eye sockets, a feature more typical of apes than of humans.

The limb bones were puzzling, too, because they were much thicker than any human arm or leg bones Fuhlrott had ever seen. Moreover, the leg bones

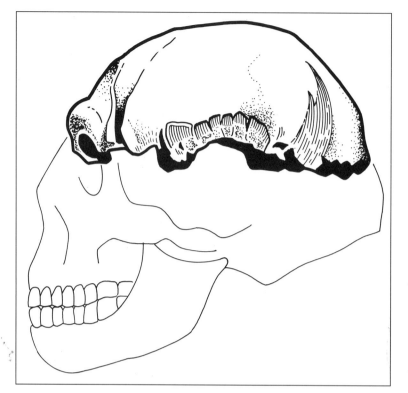

Few people could imagine the importance of the Neandertal skullcap discovered in a German river valley in 1856—three years before Darwin published his theory of evolution.

were curved, as if the being had been bowlegged. Fuhlrott was convinced the bones were human, but they were so unusual that he concluded they must belong to "a typical very ancient individual of the human race."

To confirm that opinion, Fuhlrott took the fossils to Professor Hermann Schaffhausen at the University of Bonn in Germany. Schaffhausen was an expert in anatomy. He examined the bones carefully and agreed with Fuhlrott's conclusion that they were human and ancient. In fact, he said that the "remarkable human remains from the Neander valley can be considered the oldest evidence we have of the early inhabitants of Europe." On February 4, 1857, Schaffhausen presented the bones and his analysis of them at a meeting of the Lower Rhine Medical and Natural History Society in Bonn.

German Scientists React

The German scientific community exploded with objections. No one wanted to believe these odd bones belonged to an ancient human ancestor. They were too deformed, too ugly to match the picture most people had of themselves and their ancestors. Moreover, the bones contradicted the belief expressed in the Bible that humans have looked exactly the same since the first day of creation. Scientists who rejected Schaffhausen's conclusions soon developed their own theories about the fossils. Most of them concluded the bones came from a diseased or deformed person who had died recently.

Professor Robert Mayer from the University of Bonn decided the bowed legs meant the person was a horseman, probably a Mongolian cossack in the

Russian cavalry. While chasing Napoleon's army through Germany in 1814, Mayer said, the cossack had become sick and crawled into the cave to die. No, said another scientist, the bowed legs were caused by childhood rickets, a softening of the bones caused by lack of vitamin D. This scientist claimed the poor person had frowned so much from the pain that the browridges had become enlarged.

As far as most people were concerned, however, the final word on the subject came from Dr. Rudolf Virchow, Germany's most renowned anatomist and pathologist (an expert in diseases). He announced that the bones were of recent date and the deformities caused by rickets in childhood, arthritis in old age, and severe blows on the head in between. Virchow was so respected that it seemed no one would disagree with him.

News Spreads to England

In 1861, Schaffhausen's work on the fossils was translated into English, and British scientists learned about Neanderthal (later changed to Neandertal) man, as the fossils had been named. The name meant "the man from the Neander Valley."

Many British scientists accepted Virchow's conclusions, but there were some whose curiosity about human origins had been aroused by Darwin's theory of evolution. These scientists were eager to examine Neandertal man for themselves. The possibility that he might be a human ancestor was exciting. And these fossils just might help them prove or disprove the theory that humans had evolved from apes.

Huxley's Studies

Of all the British scientists, Thomas Henry Huxley was perhaps most eager to discover more about human origins. Huxley was a brilliant biologist who had an intense interest in anatomy and paleontology. Between 1861 and 1863, he examined Neandertal man thoroughly, and in 1863, he published the results of his examination in a book entitled *Man's Place in Nature*.

Huxley's main purpose in examining the fossils had been to prove that humans were descended from apes. He had hoped his careful investigation would show the Neandertal bones had both ape and human characteristics. If Neandertal man proved to be half-human and half-ape, he would be a link between apes and humans. Huxley's work, however, did not reveal such a link. Nevertheless, his work laid the

English biologist Thomas Huxley's studies of Neandertal man greatly advanced science's understanding of human origins.

foundation for later fossil studies.

Huxley began his investigation by comparing the Neandertal skullcap to a collection of modern human skulls. Since every skull is different, Huxley decided to compare the Neandertal skullcap to modern skulls of varying sizes and shapes. This gave him a much more accurate picture of the differences and similarities between the Neandertal and modern humans.

He found that the Neandertal skullcap did not differ from the modern skulls any more than the modern skulls differed from each other. And the size of the Neandertal skullcap showed that it had held a brain at least as big as a modern human brain. In fact, in some of the comparisons, the Neandertal skull was bigger. Brain size, in Huxley's view, set humans apart from other creatures. Because he believed brain size was the most important criterion for defining a human, Huxley had to conclude that Neandertal man was human. Even so, he described the skullcap as "the most ape-like human skull I have ever seen."

Huxley's study set precedents for future studies of human fossils. For instance, his method of using a variety of examples to compare modern and ancient bones was adopted by other scientists. This made comparative anatomy studies more scientific. But even more important, Huxley's decision to call Neandertal man a human based primarily on his brain size set a standard for determining whether or not a fossil is human. That standard, refined by knowledge gained over the years, is still used today. But, for many years, that is perhaps the only way that examinations of Neandertal man advanced scientific knowledge.

Since Neandertal man was human but could not be proved ancient, most people dismissed him as the deformed, diseased, modern person Virchow said he was. Huxley and the other scientists of his day who believed in human evolution had to admit they had no proof hu-

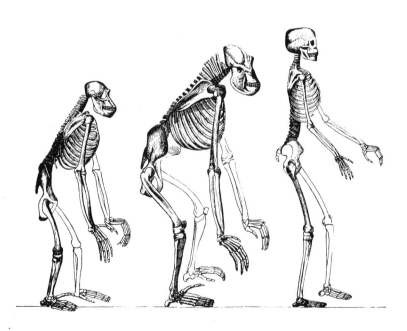

Drawings of skeletons of (left to right) a chimpanzee, a gorilla, and a human show the similarities in the anatomy of the three species.

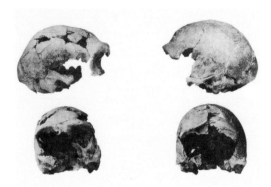

Mammal fossils and primitive stone tools found beside Neandertal skulls in a Belgian cave in 1886 enabled scientists to determine that the Neandertals lived perhaps fifty thousand years ago.

mans had evolved. Many scientists, as well as most of the general public, continued to believe in the biblical story of creation. The Neandertal fossils were ignored and forgotten for about twenty-five years.

During those years, at least two things happened that finally made Neandertal man important to the study of human origins. First, fossil-dating techniques improved, and second, more Neandertal fossils were found.

New Dating Techniques

By the late nineteenth century, paleontologists had learned a great deal about dating animal fossils. They could follow the evolutionary path of some common animals by observing fossil changes from one deposit to the next.

At the same time, geologists were learning to estimate how long each deposit took to form. This enabled them to work out a crude timetable for fossils by counting the estimated number of years in the deposits between the sur-

face and the layer where a certain animal fossil was found. Scientists could then estimate, very roughly, how long ago an animal lived. And if, for example, a fifty-thousand-year-old pig fossil was found beside human fossils and tools, the experts could be fairly certain all were approximately the same age.

More Neandertals Discovered

This new knowledge proved useful in 1886 when two fossil skeletons, very similar to Neandertal man, were discovered in a cave in Spy, Belgium. Beside those human fossils, researchers found stone tools and fossils from extinct mammals. This time, the floor of the cave was intact, and the scientists excavated it very carefully. They removed their finds slowly, layer by layer, so they would have a complete, accurate record of the exact layer and location of each fossil and tool. They carefully studied the bones. No one could argue with the conclusions. These fossils were also Neandertal, and they were very, very old, perhaps as old as 50,000 to 100,000 years.

The evidence seemed conclusive. The Neandertal fossils were definitely not from recent burials, and it was unlikely all three had the same diseases that distorted their bones in the exact same way. Now, many scientists believed they were what Fuhlrott had said they were thirty years before—members of an ancient human race.

So little was known about the Neandertals at this point that no one knew exactly what to think of them, but there was a growing suspicion they might be

Ernst Haeckel created a hypothetical creature called "speechless ape-man." He believed the creature was the missing link between apes and humans.

diagram was a picture of an actual tree with the first forms of animal life on earth, single-celled organisms, at the bottom of the trunk and humans at the top. Just below humans came apes, indicating that humans had evolved directly from apes.

By the 1880s, Haeckel and many other scientists believed apes had evolved into humans through a series of transitional creatures, each somewhat more humanlike than the one before it. That meant the older a human fossil was, the more apelike it would look. It was true that no half-ape, half-human

Haeckel's tree depicting evolution placed single-celled organisms at the base of the tree and humans at the top.

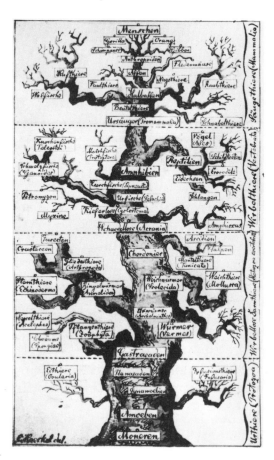

human ancestors. It now seemed possible that humans had evolved and changed. Fascinated by this idea, paleontologists developed a keen interest in finding more human fossils. This interest gave birth to a new branch of science called paleoanthropology, or the study of human origins.

Ancestral Trees

Many of these first paleoanthropologists were inclined to believe humans had evolved from apes. The many apelike characteristics of the Neandertal fossils contributed to this belief. So did the work of Ernst Haeckel, a prominent German scientist. In 1867, he had published an ancestral tree showing the evolution of all animal life on earth. He based his tree on Darwin's theory. His fossil had been found, but many pale-oanthropologists agreed with German scientist Karl Vogt, who stated:

> When it is [said] that no intermediate forms can be found, the history of the last ten years . . . tells a different tale. Twenty years ago fossil apes were unknown, and now we know of nearly a dozen . . . . Who can say that in ten, twenty or fifty years we may not possess a whole series of intermediate forms between man and ape?

Speechless Ape-Man

Because of that belief, Haeckel added a hypothetical creature he called *Pithecan-thropus alalus* (speechless ape-man) to his tree to represent the links between the unknown ape ancestor and modern humans. His idea of drawing ancestral trees soon became popular among pale-oanthropologists because it was an easily understood way to depict a theory of human origins. In a simple, graphlike picture, an ancestral tree shows the order in which species lived and the ways in which they are related.

Since Haeckel had no proof an ape-man existed, he proposed it as a theory to be investigated. However, Haeckel was so convinced an ape-man had existed, he predicted it would be found in Africa, where Darwin thought humans had originated, or in a region he called Lemuria. This region stretched from India across the Indian Ocean to Indonesia in Southeast Asia. Haeckel even hired German artist Gabriel Max to paint pictures of the creature he assumed would be found. They depict Haeckel's imaginative descriptions of

Artist Gabriel Max's rendition of Pithecanthropus alalus *shows the apelike, yet distinctly human, quality of the creatures.*

what he thought a half-ape, half-human creature would look like.

The thought of such a creature captured everyone's imagination. Instead of the series of intermediate forms Vogt had talked about, scientists were now talking about one form, an ape-man. Many people pictured it as having a human head and an ape body. Recalling the great chain of being, they began calling it the "missing link." In no time at all, most paleoanthropologists believed the answer to the mystery of human origins lay in finding this missing link. One of these scientists was a student of Haeckel's, a young Dutchman named Eugene Dubois.

The Missing Link

Eugene Dubois was the first scientist to conduct an organized search for early human fossils in the hope of unraveling the mystery of human origins. Because of his single-minded determination and phenomenal luck, his search was a success. And yet, Dubois would die feeling he had failed.

Born in the Netherlands in 1858, Dubois's childhood hobby was collecting fossils. That interest inspired him to go to medical school, where he was greatly influenced by the work of Darwin and Haeckel. After graduating in 1884, he taught anatomy at the Univer-

Dutch scientist Eugene Dubois organized the first search for the so-called missing link between apes and humans.

sity of Amsterdam. Within two years, however, his self-centered personality had antagonized his fellow professors. Unable to get along with his colleagues, Dubois resigned his position in 1887, telling everyone he was going to look for the missing link in the Dutch East Indies, which is now Indonesia.

Dubois decided to look in the East Indies based on several factors. For one thing, he agreed with Haeckel that the missing link would be found in either Africa or Southeast Asia. He explained:

> Since all apes . . . inhabit the tropics, and since the ancestors of man as they gradually lost their coat of hair will most certainly have lived in the warm areas of the earth, we are forced to conclude that the tropics is the region where we should expect to find the fossil ancestors of man.

Dubois chose to search in Asia instead of Africa because the Netherlands owned the Dutch East Indies. Dubois was unable to raise enough money for a private expedition, but he could get to the East Indies by joining his country's army medical corps.

The Search for the Missing Link

In 1887, Dubois, his wife, and his infant daughter sailed for Sumatra, one of the many Dutch East Indian islands. He had persuaded the army to give him light duty so he could devote his spare

The Solo River in central Java was the site of Dubois's celebrated find, the creature he named Pithecanthropus erectus, *or upright ape-man.*

time to searching for fossils. For two years, Dubois combed the Sumatran countryside without any luck. Then, in 1889, he contracted malaria, and the army put him on inactive duty. This left Dubois free to devote himself fully to his search, and the Dutch government cooperated by providing fifty convict laborers to help him look on the neighboring island of Java.

While his laborers excavated the sites he chose, Dubois explored Java for other possible sites. Every few weeks, the workers packed up the fossil finds in teak leaves and sent them to Dubois. Finally, in November 1890, he found, among the teak leaves, a small piece of fossilized jaw with one tooth still in place. The fragment was too small for Dubois to tell whether it came from an ape or a human, but he decided to concentrate his search near where it was found. In August 1891, his workers began digging on a fifty-foot-high bank of the Solo River near the village of Trinil.

Success on the Solo River

In September, another apelike tooth was uncovered. And less than a month after that, the workers discovered what

Dubois had been hoping for—a thick skullcap with prominent browridges. When he examined its size and shape, Dubois estimated that the brain once contained in this skull must have measured between eight hundred and one thousand cubic centimeters (cc).

Cubic centimeters had become the standard measure of brain size. Modern human brains have an average capacity of fourteen hundred cubic centimeters, whereas chimpanzee brains have an average of four hundred. So Dubois's fossil had a brain smaller than that of modern humans and larger than that of apes, but it definitely had belonged to a primate. Primates are the most highly developed animals, and this group includes apes, monkeys, and humans.

Dubois wanted to announce that the skullcap, jaw, and teeth had belonged to the missing link, but he knew those few bones were not enough evidence to convince other scientists. After examining the fossils thoroughly, he cautiously decided they had come from a chimpanzee.

In May 1892, after the winter rainy season, the work crew began digging a big trench just a few feet from where the skullcap had been found. By August, the workers had uncovered a fossil

BRAIN SIZE AND BODY WEIGHT

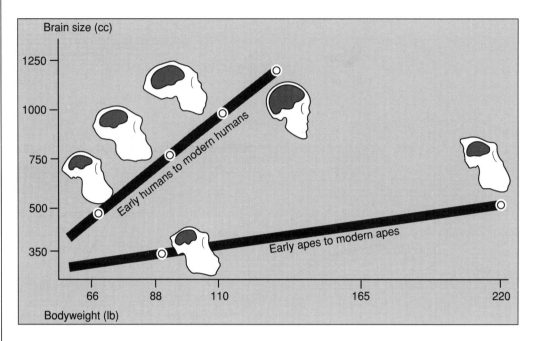

In the study of human origins, brain size is an important marker of intellectual development. Modern humans, for example, have larger brains and greater intelligence than most early humans, and many early humans had larger brains and greater intelligence than modern-day apes.

But brain size alone does not necessarily indicate level of intelligence. A large-bodied animal may have a larger brain than a smaller animal, while being no more intelligent. For this reason, scientists usually consider brain size in proportion to body weight. The relationship between brain size and body weight is called the encephalization quotient (EQ).

The chart (above) compares brain sizes and body weights of apes and members of the human family. The steep rise from ancestral humans to modern humans shows that brain size outpaced growth in body weight. The gentle rise for apes shows that their larger brains only kept pace with increases in body weight.

thighbone. Dubois concluded from the thighbone's shape that its owner had walked totally upright, but Dubois did not announce that the bone was human. Humans were then thought to be the only creatures that always walk erect. Dubois knew this, but he was hoping his fossils would be more apelike.

He wanted to find Haeckel's ape-man. He wanted to find the missing link. So, although he knew modern chimpanzees cannot walk totally erect, Dubois concluded his fossils had belonged to an extinct chimpanzee.

In October, another tooth was found. But that was it. Although the

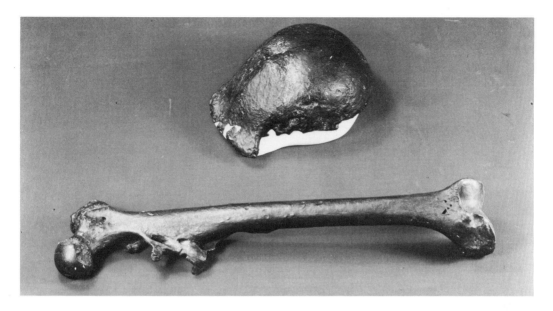

Eugene Dubois claimed that this skullcap and thigh bone belonged to the fabled missing link. Most scientists disagreed with him and pronounced the bones to be those of either an ape or a primitive human, not of the part ape-part human creature Dubois sought.

workers continued to dig through the 1893 season, no more primate fossils turned up. Dubois stopped the search and began writing a scientific paper on his chimpanzee fossils.

Partway through his writing, in 1894, Dubois suddenly changed his mind about the fossils. He so badly wanted to find the missing link that he convinced himself he had. Dubois decided the fossils had to be from Haeckel's ape-man, and he named them *Pithecanthropus erectus* (upright ape-man)

Dubois Announces His Discovery

Dubois announced his find by writing: "*Pithecanthropus erectus* is the transitional form which according to the theory of descent must have existed between man and ape. He is the [direct ancestor] of

man." Trying to prove this to the world became Dubois's lifelong obsession.

Dubois began by telegraphing the news to the Netherlands. In August 1895, Dubois returned home. That same year, he described his fossils and their discovery at the Third International Congress of Zoology in Leiden in the Netherlands. Rudolf Virchow presided over the meeting.

Scientific Objections

After Dubois's presentation, the scientists at the meeting debated the nature of the fossils. Some scientists argued that they were ape bones. Others said they were human. Haeckel was one of the few scientists who agreed with Dubois that this was the missing link.

"Now the state of affairs in this great battle for truth has been radically al-

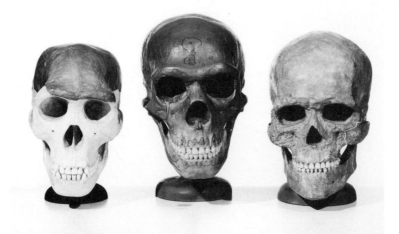

The skulls of Java man (left), Neandertal man (center) and Cro-Magnon, an early species of modern humans, (right) illustrate the evolutionary differences in jaw, brow, and brain development.

tered," Haeckel said. "Eugene Dubois' discovery of the fossil *Pithecanthropus erectus* has actually provided us with the bones of the ape-man I had postulated. This find is more important to anthropology than the much-lauded discovery of the X-ray was to physics."

Virchow, who was still very influential, disagreed with Dubois and Haeckel. He proclaimed the fossils came from more than one individual. The skull, Virchow said, "must belong to an ape. In my opinion this creature was an animal, a giant gibbon, in fact. The thighbone has not the slightest connection with the skull." He declared the thighbone came from a modern human. This was a persuasive argument because Dubois could not prove the fossils had come from one individual. He had not even been at the Solo River when they were found.

Another formidable argument against Dubois's conclusion was the belief, held by most scientists, that humans had developed a big brain long before they walked upright. Yet, this creature, if the bones were from just one individual, had walked upright and had a small brain. If this were true, sci-

entific theories of human origins and development would have to be revised. Few scientists were willing to rewrite their theories based on the scanty evidence presented by Dubois.

The meeting closed with the scientists still in disagreement about the nature of Dubois's fossils. Dubois could not accept these inconclusive results. For three years, he carried his fossils to meetings all over Europe, but he never found support for his conclusion that he had found the missing link.

Java Man

Finally, Dubois took his fossils to Arthur Keith in England. Keith was fast becoming the world's most prominent anatomist. Keith agreed with Dubois that the fossils were probably all from the same individual. Then, he dashed Dubois's hopes by saying the bones were not from the missing link, nor were they from an ape. They were from a primitive human being.

Keith was among the few scientists willing to believe early humans might have had a small brain, and he decided the skullcap was big enough to be called human. A few years later, in the early twentieth century, Keith decided 750cc was the minimum brain size a fossil must have to be considered human. This figure was accepted by most scientists, as were his conclusions about Dubois's fossils.

Dubois had nowhere else to turn. In 1898, he accepted a poorly paid teaching position at the University of Amsterdam. As his anger and bitterness grew, he withdrew more and more from the scientific community. Eventually, he also withdrew his fossils—which were now called Java man—so no one could examine them and tell him again that he was wrong. It is said he hid the bones under the floor of his dining room for many years.

Missing Link Is Discovered

One of the reasons Dubois could not convince anyone he had found the missing link was that by 1912, most scientists thought it had already been found. In 1912, Charles Dawson, a British lawyer

and amateur archaeologist, claimed to have found pieces of a skull in a gravel pit near Piltdown Common in Sussex, England. Soon, more pieces showed up, including a lower jaw and teeth. When the fossil was reconstructed, it had the large-brained skull of a modern human and humanlike teeth, but the jaw was definitely that of an ape.

At first, many scientists thought the skull and jaw could not possibly belong

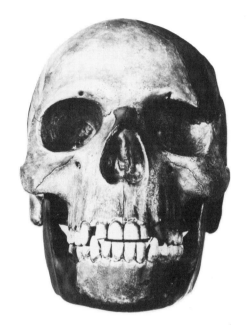

Charles Dawson (far left) and assistants sift through the English earth in search of fossils. Dawson claimed to have found the missing link, which he called Piltdown man (above). Though skeptical at first, many scientists eventually came to believe Dawson had indeed found the missing link.

together. But Piltdown man, as it was called, was actually just what scientists were looking for: an ancestor who was half-human and half-ape and had a large brain. Brushing aside their doubts, almost all the world's prominent scientists pronounced Piltdown man the missing link.

The discovery of the missing link should have solved the mystery of human origins. Very few scientists still doubted that humans had evolved from apes. But too many paleoanthropologists had begun to suspect the mystery was not that simple, especially since the role Java man and the Neandertals had played in human ancestry was still unexplained. It seemed possible Karl Vogt had been right and that instead of one missing link, there might have been a number of transitional forms between apes and modern humans.

Curious scientists wanted to examine Java man to learn more about him, but not until 1923 was Dubois persuaded to show the fossils again. To his dismay, new examinations led to the same conclusions. Java man was again pronounced human. Dubois disagreed. He had built his whole life around the discovery of the missing link, and he was not about to change his mind now. He even refused to rethink his position when, three years later, researchers in China announced the discovery of undeniably human fossils that looked very much like Java man.

Fossils Found in China

Between 1921 and 1923, a Swedish-sponsored dig near Peking in eastern China uncovered two fossilized human teeth. Photographs and descriptions of the

The dig site at Chou K'ou Tien in China yielded fossils from about forty different early humans. These became known as Peking man.

teeth were made public in 1926. The teeth belonged to a human nicknamed Peking man, and newspapers proclaimed that this was the oldest human ever found. Although very little information could be gleaned from the teeth, they caused great enthusiasm in the scientific community and the public.

Among the scientists most excited by the discovery was Davidson Black. Black was a Canadian professor of anatomy teaching at Peking Union Medical College. Within days, he had arranged for funding to reopen the digs at Chou K'ou Tien, where the two teeth had been found. The digging began in April 1927, and a third, similar tooth was found on October 16.

A German colleague later described what happened next:

> It was a remarkable tooth. Black had never seen anything like it. He made a detailed comparison of this tooth with human and [ape] teeth and came to the conclusion that it was a relic of a hitherto unknown fossil man, whom he designated *Sinanthropus pekinensis* [Chinaman from Peking]. It was certainly audacious to label a new prehistoric man on the basis of this one tooth. But Black felt justified in doing so.

Most scientists disagreed with Black. They felt it was impossible to tell anything about a creature from one tooth. Certainly, one tooth could add nothing to knowledge about human origins.

A Broken Skullcap

But luck was on Black's side. In December 1928, half a lower jaw containing three teeth was found. A year later, on December 2, 1929, at 4:00 P.M., Pei Weng Chung, the Chinese leader of the excavation, and two workers were down inside a narrow, one-hundred-foot-deep hole they had dug in the cave. Suddenly, they spotted a broken skullcap lying half in loose dirt and half in hard clay. The sun was setting, and the hole was getting dark, but they were too excited to wait until morning to dig out the skullcap. Carefully and slowly, they chipped the pieces of the skullcap loose from the clay. The skullcap turned out to be thick, long, and narrow, with a low forehead and big browridges.

Over the next several years, fourteen more skulls or parts of skulls, as well as jaws, teeth, thighbones, upper arm bones, and one wrist bone turned up in the cave. Black hoped these finds would support his earlier, and somewhat hasty, announcement of a new human species. But even Black had to admit that Peking man's skulls, teeth, and thighbones were amazingly similar to those of Java man. Partly because of Dubois's refusal to offer Java man's bones for examination, scientists ignored this coincidence for a number of years.

Altogether, the Peking man fossils represented about forty individuals whose estimated age was more than

The restored skull of Sinanthropus pekinensis, *Peking man, looks very much like that of Java man. This would later prove to be more than a coincidence.*

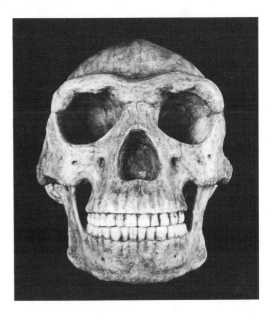

500,000 years. They were the oldest early humans known to date.

It was an exciting time for paleoanthropologists who had waited so long for this wealth of human fossils. After seeing the fossils for the first time, Roy Chapman Andrews, an American paleontologist, summed up this excitement by saying: "There it was, the skull of an individual who had lived half a million years ago, one of the most important discoveries in the whole history of human evolution! He couldn't have been very impressive when he was alive, but dead and fossilized he was awe-inspiring."

Scientists were especially excited about the knowledge they would gain from studying the large population of this new human species and its living site. The wide variety of fossils would give them the opportunity to formulate theories about who these ancient humans were and how they lived. This would be a huge step forward in knowledge about human origins.

More Fossils from Java

Peking man would make at least one other important contribution. It would help tie up the loose ends created by other finds, including Dubois's Java man. This happened in the 1930s. German explorer and paleoanthropologist Gustav Heinrich Ralph von Koenigswald discovered human fossils and tools made from flakes of stone in Java, along the Solo River, the same river where Dubois had found Java man.

Von Koenigswald was astonished to see many similarities between his flake tools and those made by Peking man. Nor could he help but notice the similarities between his Javanese fossils and the Peking man fossils. What is more, one of von Koenigswald's skulls was almost identical to Dubois's Java man skull. Von Koenigswald and Franz Weidenreich, a German anatomist who had examined Peking man thoroughly, studied all these similarities for several

A university student pieces together skull fragments found at the Chou K'ou Tien site. The site provided a wealth of materials for study.

PEKING MAN

The fossils discovered in a cave near Chou K'ou Tien, China, in the 1920s revealed a great deal about how one group of early human ancestors lived. These fossils, known collectively as Peking man, stood between five and six feet tall. They towered over their ancestors, most of whom were scarcely four feet tall. They also were burly, weighing between 90 and 160 pounds.

More importantly, Peking man possessed a relatively large brain. Measuring 1075 cubic centimeters (cc), the brain size of Peking man approached the 1400cc average identified with modern humans.

From deposits in the cave, scientists found that Peking man sought shelter there, rather than living in the open as earlier human ancestors did. He used fire to warm himself and keep away predators. It is not known whether Peking man made these fires, or simply kept them burning after they started naturally. Peking man also may have been the first human ancestor to roast meat before

eating it. Scorch marks on animal bones found in the cave suggest this was the case.

Hand-sculpted bones, antlers, and stones scattered through the cave near Chou K'ou Tien show that Peking man made a variety of tools. Ends of bones had been sharpened to points for hunting. The blunt ends of antlers were shaped into simple grips. Sharpened rocks were used for cutting, scraping, and chopping.

The state of Peking man skulls found near Chou K'ou Tien caused anthropologists to wonder if the stone tools had been used for another practice—ritual cannibalism. The holes in the base of the skulls were enlarged in a way that would have made it easy to extract the brain. Since some human groups have been known to eat human brains, a few scientists conclude that Peking man may have done so as well. Others disagree. They believe the fragile skull bases simply broke during the long periods the Peking man fossils lay buried.

English scientists debate Piltdown man's authenticity. After forty years of doubt scientists developed new techniques that proved Piltdown man was a fraud.

years. Eventually, the two scientists announced that the similarities between von Koenigswald's fossil, Dubois's Java man, and Black's Peking man were no coincidence. All three represented the same type of early human. They named this early human *Pithecanthropus erectus.*

This settled the matter for just about everyone except Dubois. When he died in 1941, Dubois was still bitterly trying to prove that Java man, not Piltdown man, was the missing link. By that time, however, many scientists were seriously doubting the existence of the missing link. They suspected Piltdown man was phony, but they had no way to prove it.

The Piltdown Fraud

The proof came in 1950 after the arrival of a new and more dependable fossil-dating technique. This technique measures fluorine content in fossils. Fluorine gas is present in some rocks and minerals. Where it is present, it can seep into buried bones. Fluorine dating does not give an absolute or definite age, but it can indicate whether bones found together are the same age.

In 1950, geologist Kenneth Oakley of the British Museum reported he had tested the fluorine content in the Piltdown man fossils. He had also tested every animal fossil found with Piltdown man. The presence of those extinct animal fossils at the Piltdown site had helped convince scientists that Piltdown man was ancient. They believed all the fossils were the same age. Oakley's tests revealed the animal fossils were much older than Piltdown man. Piltdown man became a mystery again. Then one day in 1953, Joseph Weiner, an anatomist at Oxford University in England, put together everything he knew about Piltdown man and decided it had been a deliberate hoax.

Weiner was right. Close reexamination of the skull showed that someone had buried a five-hundred-year-old human skull that was missing its lower jaw.

The lower jaw of an orangutan, with the teeth filed down to appear human, had been buried close to the skull. Because the skull's jaw hinges had been broken off, it was impossible to tell that the orangutan jaw did not fit into the skull correctly. All the pieces had been dipped in a chemical to darken them and make them look old. No one ever discovered who was responsible for the hoax, but one thing was clear. Piltdown man was a fake and one that had fooled scientists worldwide for forty-one years.

Finally, scientists acknowledged that there was no missing link. A half-ape, half-human creature that bridged the gap between apes and modern humans never existed. This acknowledgment cheered creationists, those who argue that God created human life exactly as explained in the Old Testament of the Bible. They believe that God created each of the world's species separately and that these species have essentially remained unchanged. The absence of a missing link, creationists claimed, strengthened their arguments against human evolution. Without a missing link, they said, the gap between apes and humans was too wide to support

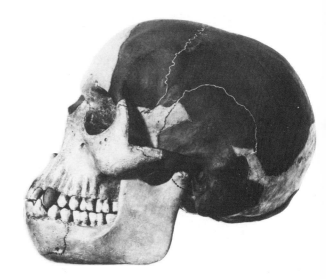

The Piltdown man skull, fabricated from human and orangutan bones, fooled scientists for decades. The perpetrator of the hoax was never discovered.

the conclusion that humans evolved from apes.

Paleoanthropologists, on the other hand, saw the gap as a challenge. They accepted that the mystery of human origins was not going to be easy to solve. The realization that there was no one missing link made most scientists more eager than ever to discover the truth about human origins.

The Leakey Bush

With Piltdown man exposed as a fraud, the missing-link theory disappeared. Scientists were relieved. Piltdown man had interfered with serious investigation of other theories. One of these other theories gained prominence in the 1950s. It postulated that a number of transitional species had existed between the ancestral ape and modern humans and that each species was more humanlike than the one before it.

All of the transitional species are called hominids. Modern humans are hominids, too. A hominid is any primate that belongs to the human family. So, the first human ancestors were hominids, but they were too apelike to be-

Raymond Dart's Taung baby, the first specimen found of Australopithecus africanus, *had both apelike and humanlike features.*

long to the genus *Homo*, that is, too apelike to be called human. Hominids would have to evolve for thousands of years before they developed the human characteristics that would place them in the genus *Homo*. Their morphology—their physical form and structure—would have to become more humanlike and their brains would have to become bigger. It would then take many more thousands of years before these early humans evolved into modern humans.

The Single-Species Theory

The most popular theory of human origins in the 1950s was the single-species theory. The theory claimed that all known extinct hominids, including Java man, Peking man, and Neandertal man, were human ancestors. According to the theory, only one species of hominid lived at any given time. Each hominid species disappeared as it evolved into the next more humanlike species.

The ancestral tree drawn to depict this theory rose in a straight line from the ancestral ape to modern humans. It showed the still-unknown ancestral ape evolving into the oldest known ancestor, an apelike hominid called *Australopithecus africanus* (southern ape of Africa). After *africanus* came the first known early human, *Pithecanthropus erectus*, now known as *Homo erectus*. This group included Java man and Peking man. Above *erectus* was Neandertal man, but it had one feature that convinced Dart it was a hominid. That feature was its foramen magnum, the skull opening through which the spinal cord passes. In apes, the foramen magnum is located at the back of the skull, as it is with all creatures that walk on four legs. The Taung baby's foramen magnum was located at the bottom of the skull, a feature found only in hominids, the only creatures that walk fully erect.

Dart did not believe the Taung baby belonged to the genus *Homo*, however. Its features were far too apelike and its brain far too small for it to be an early human. But because the Taung baby had walked erect, Dart felt it had to be a hominid, a human ancestor.

Most prominent scientists rejected Dart's conclusions. Influential anatomist Arthur Keith said, "At most, it represents a genus in the chimpanzee or gorilla group."

Dart fought for twenty-five years to have *africanus* accepted as a hominid. During those years, two things happened that finally convinced scientists he was right. First, more australopithecine fossils were found. Some of these fossils were from adults and resembled those of the Taung baby. The adults appeared to have been small, apelike creatures, perhaps three to four feet tall, and, like the Taung baby, they had walked upright.

Second, in the late 1940s, Wilford Le Gros Clark, who had replaced Keith as Great Britain's most prominent anatomist, did an exhaustive study comparing ape and human teeth. He devised a list of twelve consistent, unmistakable differences between them. Then he used that list to compare ape, human, and australopithecine teeth.

In 1950, Clark announced that aus-

An artist's rendition of Australopithecus africanus, *once thought to be the oldest human ancestor. The apelike hominid walked upright and lived about one million years ago.*

whose Latin name was *Homo neanderthalensis*. After the Neandertals came modern humans, or *Homo sapiens*.

The First Ancestor

Africanus was discovered in Taung, South Africa, in 1924 by anatomist Raymond Dart, a professor at the University of Witwatersrand in Johannesburg, South Africa. The skull Dart discovered was called the Taung baby because it came from a child. The Taung baby's features were apelike, with a jutting jaw, heavy browridges, and an ape-size brain, tralopithecine teeth resembled human teeth in all twelve ways. Most scientists took this to mean that Dart's *africanus* was a hominid, the oldest known human ancestor on the ancestral tree. Relative dating indicated that it lived about one million years ago.

Robust Australopithecines

Although some of these later australopithecine fossils were identifed as *africanus*, others were quite different. At first, scientists thought there might be as many as five different australopithecines, but by the 1950s, they had classified all the fossils into two types. The first was *africanus*, also called a gracile (gracefully slender) australopithecine. The second, called *Australopithecus robustus* (robust southern ape) or robust australopithecine, was much larger than *africanus* and more than a foot taller. It had a powerful jaw and huge teeth, and its skull had a bony crest on top where the massive jaw muscles were anchored. Almost everything about it was huge, except its brain, which was an apelike five hundred cubic centimeters.

Doubts About the Single-Species Theory

Relative-dating studies indicated that *robustus* and *africanus* had lived at approximately the same time, which made some scientists question the single-species theory. They agreed that both *africanus* and *robustus* were hominids, which meant they were both human ancestors. But according to the theory, this was impossible because each ho-

minid species was thought to have replaced the one before it. *Africanus* and *robustus* could not both be ancestors if they had lived at the same time.

Moreover, paleoanthropologists felt *robustus* could not be a human ancestor because of its morphology. The body was too massive, and its jaw and teeth too huge for it to have evolved into the small-toothed, small-jawed *Homo erectus*. Some scientists saw this as a sign that the single-species theory was wrong. It did not take long for a new theory to circulate. This new theory suggested that there could have been more than one species of hominid alive at the same time and that not all of these hominid species were necessarily human ancestors.

Revising the Ancestral Tree

Scientists pondered this idea and tried to figure out how *robustus* fit into a human ancestral tree. Maybe the tree was

An Australopithecus robustus *skull shows the powerful jaw and large teeth of this hominid.*

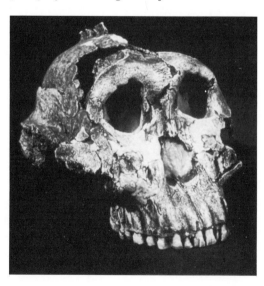

A collection of Australopithecus *skull fragments found in African caves. The discovery of different species of australopithecines who lived at the same time compelled scientists to rethink their theories of human evolution.*

not a straight trunk after all, they thought. Maybe the tree had limbs branching off the trunk, branches that represented hominids who were related to humans but had contributed nothing to human ancestry before going extinct. Maybe *robustus* was a human cousin with no direct links to human development. Maybe, some scientists thought, *robustus* was nothing more than a dead-end branch.

Not enough evidence existed at this point to tell which ancestral tree was right. Scientists would need more hominid fossils or a more definite method of dating before they could continue the investigation. Within a few years, they would have both.

The Leakey Bush

In 1959, new hominid fossils were discovered by a paleoanthropologist named Louis Leakey. Leakey, a British missionary's son, was born in 1903 in the East African country of Kenya. His persistence in working to prove his theory of human origins, along with extraordinary luck, eventually made him the most famous paleoanthropologist in the world.

Leakey believed that human origins would be traced to Africa and that the earliest humans lived six to eight million years ago. To many scientists, this time period seemed too long. To Leakey, however, it made perfect sense.

Archaeologist Mary Leakey and her husband, paleoanthropologist Louis Leakey, examine a jaw bone found in Tanzania. The find turned out to be an important piece of the human origins puzzle.

Evolution is a slow process, and Leakey could not believe it had occurred in anything less than millions of years.

Leakey also disagreed with many of his colleagues on another point. He saw no evidence to support the view that Peking man, Java man, Neandertal man, and the australopithecines were

Louis Leakey did not believe that the path of human evolution had passed through any of the known hominid species.

human ancestors. These fossil groups, Leakey said, "are really nothing but various aberrant [abnormal] and overspecialized branches that broke away at different times from the main stock leading to *Homo*." In other words, Leakey believed all the known hominids had gone extinct without contributing to human evolution.

Leakey's controversial ancestral tree, therefore, resembled a bush more than a tree. All the known hominids were on individual side branches. Since Leakey believed no human ancestors had yet been found, the center stem of his bush was empty. He devoted much of his career to finding a fossil that would prove the genus *Homo* had begun in Africa six to eight million years ago. This creature would be placed in the center stem of the human ancestral bush.

Olduvai Gorge

In order to prove his theory, Louis and his wife, Mary, an archaeologist, had been going to Olduvai Gorge in Tanzania, a country in East Africa, every dry season since the early 1930s to hunt for early human fossils. By 1959, they had

Workers labor patiently at Tanzania's Olduvai Gorge, where the Leakeys found a skull they believed belonged to a new type of human ancestor.

not found any of the fossils they were seeking, but they had found several signs that early humans had lived there.

Primitive stone tools found in several deposits offered the strongest evidence of early human activity. Most scientists agreed that the apelike hominids who preceded early humans could not have made tools from stone. They believed only hominids in the genus *Homo* made tools. The Leakeys considered the tools to be proof that early humans had lived in Olduvai, but to convince others, they needed human fossils.

On July 17, 1959, the Leakeys were camped as usual in Olduvai Gorge. On this particular morning, Louis was sick in bed, so Mary walked with her six dalmatians to a site where many tools had been found. Suddenly, she spotted an interesting looking fragment of bone

sticking out of an eroding slope. She carefully brushed away the dirt, exposing a skull. When she saw its teeth, she recognized them as hominid.

This, Mary hoped, was the tool-maker they had been seeking all these years. She rushed back to camp and told Louis, and together they returned to the site. Louis took one look at the teeth and, according to Mary, expressed great disappointment. Initially, at least, the skull looked to Louis like just another australopithecine fossil.

Leakey Finds the Oldest Human

Once the skull had been unearthed, Louis could see it lacked certain human characteristics. It was similar to *robustus*

TOOLS

Modern day stone knapper demonstrates ancient method of toolmaking.

Although chimpanzees use primitive tools, such as leaves to collect water and twigs to prod for termites, toolmaking seems to be unique to humans. That is why Louis and Mary Leakey were excited by the discovery of crude tools in the Olduvai Gorge in Tanzania. These tools, known as Oldowan tools, showed that humans had progressed beyond the simple tools used by apes. Oldowan tools were not just found by their users; they had been made.

It was clear from the findings in the Olduvai Gorge and elsewhere in Africa that early hominids used naturally sharp rocks for breaking open nuts and gourds and scraping meat off bones and hide. At some point, the hominids discovered that by striking two stones together, they could chip away small fragments, transforming a blunt stone into a sharp one. This was the first toolmaking.

Even this simple act required considerable skill and planning. The prehistoric stone cutters, or knappers, had to select rocks that would be hard enough for cutting and scraping, but fragile enough to chip and break easily. Crystal rock like quartz, flint, and chert were ideal for toolmaking. The ancient knappers then looked for existing cracks in the rocks, so they could control the breakage, obtaining a tool of a desired shape.

The sharpened rocks, known as core tools, came in many different shapes. Large stones that came to a point were used as hammers. Stones with one sharp edge were used for chopping. Disc-shaped stones with sharpened rims and other stones with three or more sharp edges were used for cutting. Flattened stones with one sharp edge were used for scraping flesh from hides. The stone flakes chipped off during the making of larger tools were used for fine cutting and scraping such as removing meat from bones.

It is possible that hominids used sticks and other soft materials as tools long before they began to use stone. Such tools, however, probably decayed eons ago.

but even more massive. Its back molars were as big around as nickels, and the brain was only about five hundred cubic centimeters. The fossil, however, had been found in a deposit dated at 600,000 years old. If Louis could somehow prove it was an early human, it would be the oldest known early human ever found. That would be a start toward proving his theory that humans were much older than other scientists suspected.

Louis wanted this so badly that he eventually convinced himself that Mary's find was indeed an early human. In his field notebook, he wrote: "He is a fabulous creation. *Titanhomo mirabilis* [miraculous giant man] would be a good name. People will say he is NOT human but he is." Louis knew scientists would never accept such a massive, small-brained creature as an early human, despite the tools that seemed to

Louis Leakey measures the cranium of the nearly two-million-year-old skull of Zinjanthropus boisei, *nicknamed Zinj.*

indicate it was the Oldowan (another name for Olduvai) toolmaker.

Louis wrestled with what to call Mary's find. He could not call it *Australopithecus* because that would be acknowledging that australopithecines were human ancestors, and Louis rejected this theory.

Louis escaped his dilemma by calling the skull neither *Homo* nor *Australopithecus*. Instead, he announced to the world his 600,000-year-old toolmaker was a new type, a new genus of human ancestor. He named it *Zinjanthropus boisei* (Boise's East African man), honoring Charles Boise, who had helped fund the Leakey's search. The fossil came to be known as Zinj.

The Zinj Controversy

Because it was said to be the oldest early human ever found, Zinj became an overnight sensation when Louis Leakey introduced it in August 1959. It made the Leakeys and Olduvai Gorge famous. The scientific community and the general public suddenly became fascinated by paleoanthropology. Louis went from one country to another, speaking and raising money for his work. People listened eagerly as he described finding "the world's earliest man."

At the same time, however, many paleoanthropologists felt Louis had made a mistake. Zinj, they said, was obviously a robust australopithecine and not some new type of human ancestor, as the Leakeys claimed. The one thing about Zinj no one doubted was his age. Within a year, however, a new dating technique would make scientists revise the age of Zinj. The outcome would surprise even Louis.

Geologist Garniss Curtis helped invent the potassium-argon fossil-dating technique used to determine Zinj's great age.

Improved Dating Techniques

In 1960, less than a year after Zinj was discovered, geologists Garniss Curtis and Jack Evernden at the University of California at Berkeley introduced a new fossil-dating technique. Called potassium-argon dating, this technique did not give relative dates or estimates. It gave absolute dates. For the first time, paleoanthropologists had a dating method that enabled them to determine the actual age of a fossil.

The technique, however, applies only to fossils found in volcanic rock. Volcanic rock contains the chemical potassium, which decays slowly and regularly over millions of years. In the pro-

cess, it changes into argon gas. This change begins as the rock deposit forms, which means scientists can determine the age of the deposit by measuring the amount of argon present in the rock. Any fossils found in the deposit would have the same age.

Because much of the rock in Olduvai Gorge is volcanic, Curtis and Evernden were able to test their new technique on Zinj. When they did, they found that Zinj was not 600,000 years old as the Leakeys had thought. Potassium-argon dating placed Zinj's age at 1.75 million years old.

The Leakeys could not have been happier. Suddenly, their fossil had more than tripled the previously known age of early humans. Louis was more convinced than ever that his theory was right, and he expected his colleagues to now support him. That did not happen. Too many scientists still believed that Zinj was a robust australopithecine and not a human ancestor. Only the gracile australopithecine, *africanus*, was considered a human ancestor.

If those scientists were right, then Louis would be back where he started with no fossil to support his theory. Within a few years, the Leakeys' own sons would discover new fossils that would prove these skeptics right. Zinj was a robust australopithecine. But Louis did not have to worry about his error for long because the fossils his sons found turned out to be the real toolmaker from Olduvai Gorge.

The Toolmaker

The controversy over Zinj caused an uproar in paleoanthropology, but that did not last long. In 1960, within months after Louis had announced the discovery of Zinj, the Leakeys' oldest son, Jonathon, proved he also had the Leakey luck. Jonathon found a new fossil at Olduvai, and this time it really was a 1.75-million-year-old early human. This new human ancestor, named *Homo habilis* (handy man), was also controversial, but it would eventually take its place on the human ancestral tree. As a result, the Leakeys caused a small revolution in paleoanthropology. That revolution accomplished two things. It caused most scientists to reject the single-species theory, and it completed the transformation of ancestral trees into bushes.

Jonny's Child

The revolution began in May 1960, when Jonathon, then nineteen, was wandering alone around the site where Zinj had been found. He spotted a bone protruding from a slope. The bone turned out to be the lower jaw of a saber-toothed tiger, a rare find. While sieving the dirt in search of more tiger fossils, Jonathon came across a hominid tooth and finger bone. The tiger was quickly forgotten, and a search for the source of the hominid fossils began.

On June 13, Jonathon found a hominid collarbone and several thin pieces of skull. Eventually, the Leakeys gathered a strange assortment of 2,158 fossils, including hominid hand bones, foot bones, skull fragments, and a jaw with the teeth still in place.

Later, similar fossils, along with Oldowan tools, were discovered at three other sites. From all these pieces, the Leakeys were able to identify four hominids. The first one, named Jonny's child in honor of its discoverer, was a juvenile consisting of a lower jaw and two skull fragments.

The lower jawbone of a 1.75-million-year-old hominid named Jonny's child was evidence of a new human ancestor.

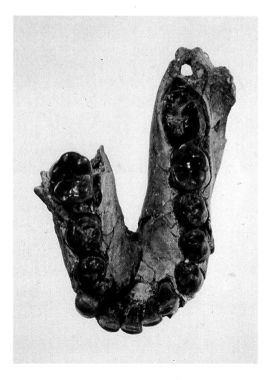

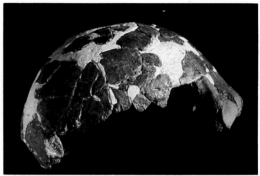

These skull fragments, a lower and upper jaw (left) and a reconstructed skullcap, belong to Cindy and George, respectively, two of the three other hominids found along with Jonny's child in Olduvai Gorge.

The other three were named Cindy, Twiggy, and George. Cindy (short for Cinderella) consisted of a lower jaw and teeth, pieces of an upper jaw, and a bit of skull. Twiggy, named after a skinny fashion model of the 1960s, was a flattened skull and seven teeth. George consisted of some teeth and a few small pieces of skull.

As he pieced together an image from the fossil fragments, Louis Leakey saw an early human being emerge. Other than age, these fossils had nothing in common with Zinj. The teeth were small, the face was flat without an apelike jutting jaw, the skull was thin and delicate, and the forehead was high, not sloping. The fossils, Louis concluded, had to have come from the early humans he had been looking for.

Proving the Fossils Human

Rather than make an immediate announcement, as he had done with Zinj, Louis and his team of experts studied the fossils, tools, and other evidence collected at the sites. Their study lasted four years. It produced encouraging physical and cultural evidence to support their theory.

This group of hominids appeared to possess an important human trait: the ability to plan ahead. Their tools had been chipped from stone found at least eight miles away. This indicated the toolmakers had searched for the best rock rather than simply using what was readily available.

Physically, the fossils resembled early humans in most respects. The teeth met Clark's twelve-point test. The hands had opposable thumbs, which are thumbs able to touch each of the four fingertips. Fully opposable thumbs permit a grasp tight enough to manipulate things with precision. A being with opposable thumbs has the physical ability to make and use tools. A foot reconstructed from the fossil pieces indicated these beings had walked upright.

The only feature that did not seem human was the brain. Skulls reconstructed from many tiny fragments indicated that the brains of these beings had averaged only about 650cc. That was 100cc less than the standard 750cc for the genus *Homo*. Since brain size was considered the most important factor in determining whether or not a fossil is human, this exception was enough to cast doubt on Leakey's conclusion that these fossils came from early humans.

To eliminate this doubt, Leakey and his team reworked the criteria for the genus *Homo*. Generally, the changes they made were justified, and most still apply today. Aside from lowering the minimum brain size to six hundred cubic centimeters, Leakey and his team concluded that a member of the genus *Homo* must walk erect and must have a thin-boned skull with a high forehead, a flat face without a jutting jaw, and opposable thumbs.

Leakey's Announcement

On April 4, 1964, Leakey announced to the world that he had discovered the real toolmaker, a new 1.75-million-year-old human ancestor called *Homo habilis*. He also admitted he had been wrong about Zinj. Although Zinj had lived at the same time as *habilis*, Zinj was not a human ancestor or the Oldowan toolmaker. Zinj was a robust australopithecine, and its name was changed to *Australopithecus boisei*.

Despite Leakey's precautions, most paleoanthropologists reacted to his announcement with disbelief. They agreed *habilis* was a hominid as well as a human ancestor. They even agreed on its age. But they were not at all sure it belonged in the genus *Homo*. They questioned whether *Homo habilis* really could be considered an early human. Some doubted Leakey's new criteria for determining if fossils were from humans. Many said that it would be more appropriate to call this being *Australopithecus*.

The creationists agreed with the pa-leoanthropologists on this point. They also concluded that *habilis* was an australopithecine. The two groups split here, however, since the creationists believed australopithecines were apes, not hominids. According to this view, Leakey's new creature was an extinct ape and had nothing to do with human ancestry.

Leakey brushed aside most of the criticism and controversy. He was convinced that *habilis* belonged in the genus *Homo* and that this species represented the only human ancestor then known to science.

Advancing age and failing health prevented Leakey from continuing his search for evidence to prove this theory. Although he continued to travel the world, charming audiences with his tales, *Homo habilis* was his last important

The flattened skull of Twiggy, the fourth hominid found along with Jonny's child in Olduvai Gorge.

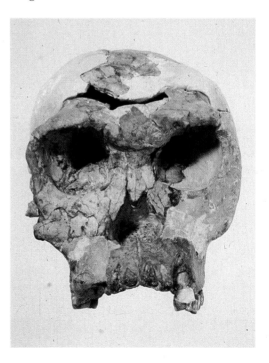

Turkana fishermen near the site where Richard Leakey's fossil hunters found 300 tiny skull pieces. When reconstructed, the skull was known only by its museum number, 1470.

fossil discovery. But the Leakey name did not lose its close association with the search for human origins. By the time of Louis Leakey's death, another son, Richard, was already carrying on the Leakey tradition.

As a child, Richard had never shown an interest in his parents' activities. As a result, he did not have a formal education in paleoanthropology or any related field. However, he had great organizational skills, a keen eye for fossil de-

Richard Leakey examines Zinj, later classified as Australopithecus boisei. *Richard's discoveries were as controversial as those of his parents.*

posits, and the Leakey luck. His interest in fossils began in 1967 when, at the age of twenty-two, he organized the Kenyan contingent of an international fossil-hunting expedition to Ethiopia. In 1972, a few days before Louis died, Richard was able to show his father a new skull he had just discovered. It looked much like *habilis* and had an astounding potassium-argon date of 2.9 million years. "It's marvelous," Louis told Richard. "But they won't believe you."

Discovery of 1470

Richard's skull, still known by its museum number, 1470, definitely belonged to the genus *Homo*. Although the face was primitive, with browridges, a flat nose, and slightly jutting jaws, the skull was thin-boned and had a high forehead, and it was big. Its brain size had been measured at 775cc, large enough to satisfy most scientists. Yet Richard's discovery became the center of a controversy as big as any Louis had ever encountered.

The road to that discovery began in 1967. That year, while flying over the eastern shore of Lake Turkana in northern Kenya, Richard decided that the hot, windy, desolate terrain was perfect for fossil hunting. In 1969, he received funding for an expedition to the area, which is called Koobi Fora.

Leakey took a team of experts with him, including geologists who began the complicated task of dating the deposits. One of those geologists, Kay Behrensmeyer, found Oldowan tools in a tuff, or volcanic deposit. As was the custom, the tuff came to be known as the Kay Behrensmeyer Site (KBS) tuff. Behrensmeyer sent rock samples from the tuff off for dating, and the report came back saying that the deposit was 2.6 million years old. Leakey was elated.

Like his father, he believed early humans were very ancient. If the dating was correct, these were the oldest tools ever found, and that meant early humans had to be at least the same age.

Over the next ten years, Leakey's team of fossil hunters—known as the Hominid Gang—uncovered about five thousand hominid and other fossils. Among these were 300 tiny hominid skull pieces that would come to be known as 1470. Leakey's zoologist wife, Meave, and anatomist Alan Walker built an almost complete skull from these pieces over several months. Because the skull pieces were found beneath the KBS tuff, their age was estimated at 2.9 million years old.

Geologist Kay Behrensmeyer (left) indicates the large back teeth in a skull found in a volcanic deposit (right) on the shore of Lake Turkana. As is the custom, the deposit was named after her because she was the first person to find primitive tools there.

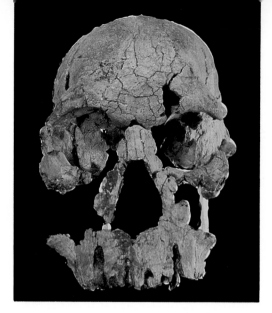

The reconstructed skull of Homo habilis, *the tool-making human, known only as 1470.*

Habilis Brain Reveals Secrets

Among the scientists who studied the reconstructed skull was Columbia University biologist Ralph Holloway. Holloway studies the brains of extinct hominids by making latex casts of the insides of fossil skulls. The cast shows the brain's imprint on the fossilized skull. The imprint enables Holloway to study the brain's form and shape. From its form and shape, and various lines and bulges, Holloway can analyze the level of the brain's development.

Holloway compared australopithecine casts with the brain cast from 1470. Of the two, 1470's brain appeared to have a more humanlike shape and proportions. The part of the brain that controls speech was bigger, or at least more complex in 1470. In fact, it was big and complex enough to indicate that 1470 might have been capable of speech. But the main difference involved the area of the brain that controls the ability to use the hands. That area was considerably larger in 1470, big enough to confirm that the creature was most likely a toolmaker.

1470 Becomes Controversial

Many scientists believed 1470 was *habilis*. But *habilis* was still controversial and poorly defined, and Leakey was not certain, so he did not announce the skull's species. When it came to naming it, he said, "I will merely call it *Homo.*" He was willing, however, to announce that he had found the oldest early human. This brought him instant fame at the age of twenty-eight.

Almost immediately, Leakey's enjoyment of that fame was marred by hints that 1470 was not as old as he claimed.

Ralph Holloway works on a cast of a skull. Holloway's cast of 1470 supported the theory that Homo habilis *made and used tools.*

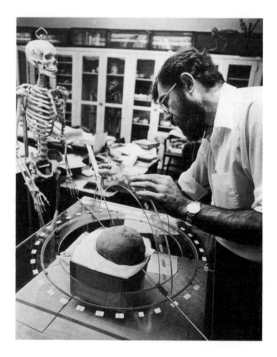

BRAIN IMPRINTS

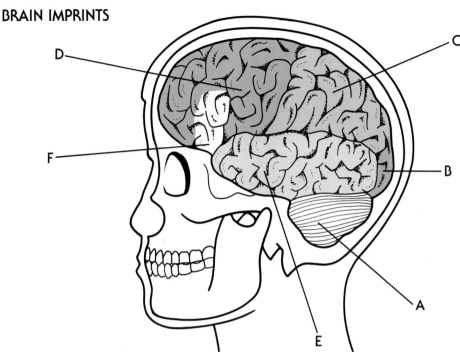

Columbia University biologist Ralph Holloway realized in the 1970s that the imprint made by the brain on the inside of the skull could be used to study hominid development. This is because the brain physically changes as it becomes more complex and the functions it governs become more highly developed. The changes can be seen in the lines and bulges imprinted on the skull.

Scientists like Holloway make casts of the insides of fossilized skulls to obtain these imprints. Researchers look for imprinted patterns made by the cerebellum (A), which governs muscular coordination; the occipital lobe (B), which controls vision; the parietal lobe (C), which processes sensory information; the frontal lobe (D), which controls movement; the temporal lobe (E), which is the seat of memory; and Broca's area (F), which is the center for speech.

Imprints have shown that many early hominids have a brain pattern distinctly different from that of apes. Like modern humans, many early hominids had less developed occipital lobes and thus more limited vision than apes. Early hominids also had larger temporal and parietal lobes than apes, which indicates that they had greater memory and general body awareness.

After the initial test on the KBS tuff, a number of others had been run, and the results had varied widely.

Eventually, Leakey had to admit that his fossil was somewhere between 1.8 and 2 million years old, not 2.9 million years old as he had hoped. The 1470 fossil would not bring the Leakeys any closer to proving humans were 6 to 8 million years old. However, it was the finest example of *Homo habilis* yet found, and *habilis* could now take its place as the first of the early humans.

This and other Leakey discoveries

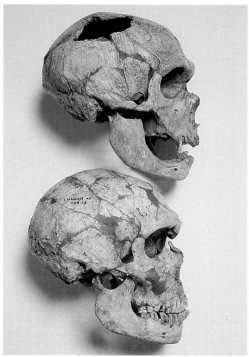

In the photo at left (clockwise from left) are skulls of Homo habilis, Australopithecus robustus, *and* Australopithecus africanus. *On the right are two Neandertal skulls. Evidence that more than one hominid species lived at the same time disproved the single-species theory.*

caused paleoanthropologists to revise their theories again. They discarded the single-species theory because the Leakeys had proved that two hominids—*Australopithecus boisei* (Zinj) and *Homo habilis*—had lived at the same time. Plus, with Zinj relegated to a side branch along with *Australopithecus robustus*, the human ancestral tree became—once and for all—a bush.

Moreover, scientists now believed that Neandertal man also belonged on a side branch. Improved dating techniques indicated that the Neandertals had not gone extinct until about thirty thousand years ago, while the first modern humans had appeared about forty thousand years ago. If the Neandertals and modern humans had indeed lived side by side for ten thousand years, the Neandertals could not have evolved into modern humans as was previously thought.

As these theories developed, the main stem of the human ancestral bush began to take shape. According to the most widely accepted theory of the 1970s, *africanus* (Taung baby), who was more apelike than human, belonged at the root of the main stem. *Habilis*, believed to be the first early human, came next, followed by *erectus* (Java man and Peking man). Finally, *Homo sapiens*, the modern humans, were at the top. In just a short time, however, the discovery of a new human ancestor would cause scientists to revise their theories yet again.

The Oldest Human Ancestor

By the 1970s, despite all the knowledge that had been gained, human origins seemed even more of a mystery than before. Now, paleoanthropologists not only had to discover the identity of human ancestors but they also had to untangle the relationships between these ancestors and the other hominids. It appeared that the first step was to find the oldest hominid. Then, scientists would at least know their starting point. That might make it easier to figure out how the various hominids had evolved and why some became human ancestors and others did not.

Soon, Africa was dotted with fossil-

hunting expeditions looking for the oldest hominid. Donald Johanson, a thirty-one-year-old American paleoanthropologist, co-led one of them. Johanson had decided to hunt in a place called Hadar in the Afar region of northeastern Ethiopia. Despite its arid badlands and tormenting heat, Hadar is an ideal place to hunt for hominid fossils. Three or possibly four million years ago, the area was a lake that attracted hominids because they wanted to live along its shore. So in 1973 and 1974, Johanson and his colleagues busily began mapping, dating, and searching the area.

American paleoanthropologist Donald Johanson studies a fossil at a dig site. Johanson and a student assistant discovered Lucy, a three-million-year-old hominid, in Ethiopia.

Johanson's Discovery

On the morning of November 30, 1974, Johanson planned to stay in camp to do paperwork. But when Tom Gray, an American graduate student, asked him about the location of site 162, Johanson decided to show him where it was. After two uneventful hours of surveying the site, they headed back toward camp.

On the way, they passed through a small gully. It had been searched several times with no results, but Johanson was feeling lucky and thought a quick look might be worthwhile. As usual, the gully seemed empty of fossils, but just as Johanson was turning to leave, he spotted something on the slope. When he knelt to examine it, he saw it was a hominid arm bone. Suddenly, the slope seemed alive with hominid bones: the back of a skull, jawbones, a thighbone, a couple of vertebrae, part of a pelvis, and ribs. Johanson could not be certain, but he had a feeling he had found something important.

Johanson said later:

> For a while we just groped around from one bone to the next, too stunned to speak. It occurred to me right away that perhaps all these bones might belong to a single individual. But I was afraid to speak that thought out loud, as if by doing so I would break the spell, and we would once again find ourselves standing in an unremarkable boneless little gully in the middle of nowhere. Tom, on the other hand, could not hold in his excitement. He let out a yell, and then I heard myself yelling too, and we were hugging each other and dancing up and down in the heat.

The next day, everyone in camp returned to the site to begin the task of collecting every piece of bone they could find. The search took three weeks. When it was done, they had about two hundred fossil pieces that represented about 40 percent of a single skeleton. From the pelvis, Johanson and his team could tell that the fossils were from a female. They named her Lucy after the Beatles' song *Lucy in the Sky with Diamonds*, which played over and over in camp that night.

The Lucy Puzzle

There were three things about Lucy that made her special. First, these fossils were a new type, different from anything ever found before. Lucy was definitely a hominid because her hip and leg bones indicated that she had walked erect. But her skull was small, not much bigger than a softball, and her brain capacity could not have been more than about 410cc. She was short, perhaps 3.5 feet tall, and had short legs and long arms. Her face was apelike, with a low forehead, prominent browridges, a flat nose, and jutting jaws. In fact, she must have looked similar to a slender chimpanzee, except that her hands and teeth were humanlike. Because her wisdom teeth had erupted, she probably was about twenty when she died.

The second thing that made Lucy

Lucy reconstructed. Lucy was unique among previously found hominids because of her age and because her skeleton was so complete. She was also special because she represented a new hominid species.

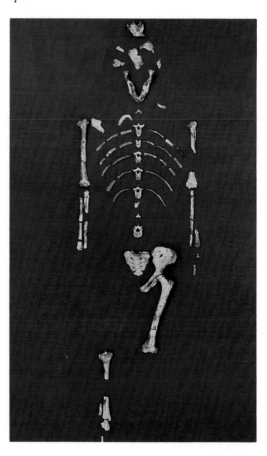

special was the completeness of her skeleton. No one had ever found so many pieces of such a primitive hominid skeleton. This time, no one had to guess what the new hominid looked like. Lucy's bones could speak for themselves. The third and most amazing thing about Lucy was her age. Potassium-argon dating showed that she had died three million years ago. This made her the oldest known hominid.

But what kind of hominid was she? Johanson wrestled with this question for some time, finally deciding that she was either a small member of the genus *Homo* or a small australopithecine. Her size and features continued to baffle him. "Much as I wanted to believe that Lucy was human," Johanson said, "I couldn't bring myself to accept anything so small and apparently primitive as *Homo*."

The First Family

In 1975, while he was still trying to decide what genus Lucy belonged to, Johanson made another important discovery. Not far from where Lucy had been found, he spotted a collection of hominid fossils. There were jaws, teeth, leg bones, hand and foot bones, ribs, vertebrae, and skull fragments—197 pieces in all. When the pieces were sorted, Johanson had thirteen individuals: men, women, juveniles, and infants. Although many scientists doubted they were actually a family, the group became known as the First Family.

Johanson studied the First Family fossils. The teeth had some humanlike qualities. The hand and foot bones were almost identical to those of modern humans. Although there were no

Donald Johanson and colleagues pose with the complete collection of fossils found at the Hadar site, including the bones of First Family.

skulls complete enough to judge brain size, one jaw definitely looked like a *habilis* jaw. Potassium-argon dating had placed the age of these fossils at about three million years.

As Johanson considered these bits of evidence, he began to develop a theory. Perhaps the First Family belonged to the genus *Homo*, which would mean they were the oldest early humans ever found. When primitive stone tools were discovered nearby the following year and dated at 2.6 million years, Johanson's suspicion was strengthened.

As Johanson's work at Hadar progressed, so did Mary Leakey's search in

LUCY

The 1974 discovery of the fossil known as Lucy provided a new direction for the study of human origins. Aside from being the most complete primitive hominid skeleton found until that time, Lucy represented a new hominid species as well as the oldest known human ancestor to date.

Despite her age, and because 40 percent of her skeleton was intact, scientists were able to piece together a great deal about who Lucy was and how she lived. Scarcely four feet tall, Lucy probably weighed only about sixty pounds. Her slender body was topped by a small, chimpanzeelike head. She was covered with fur—brown, black, reddish, or even silver. The skin that showed on her palms, chest, and face was probably dark, as it is on most creatures in hot, sunny climates.

Lucy's arms were proportionately longer than a modern human's, and her long fingers curved inward. These ape-like proportions led some scientists to conclude that Lucy may have slept in trees to avoid predators. Other scientists disagreed. They looked at her feet and said they could not be used for grasping tree limbs. They believed she had come down from the trees for good.

The shape of Lucy's feet, legs, hips, and backbone show that she walked upright. Her teeth also yielded information about how she lived. Her molars were flat, ideal for grinding seeds and grains. This led some scientists to conclude that she was a vegetarian although later tests showed that she probably also ate meat. Her chipped front teeth were a sign that she used her teeth as tools. This implied that she did not make her own tools out of sticks or rocks.

Although scientists learned much from Lucy, her aged skeleton is not likely to yield more secrets. Further information about her species will probably have to come from other fossils.

Tanzania. In 1974, the Leakeys were having a Christmas picnic at a desolate place called Laetoli, just twenty-five miles south of Olduvai. There, on the ground, Mary and another Leakey son, Philip, spotted several hominid fossils, including teeth, a juvenile jaw, and an adult jaw. Their potassium-argon date proved to be 3.7 million years, older than Johanson's fossils.

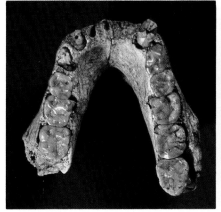
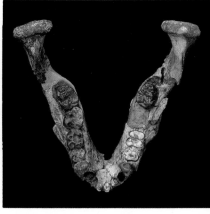

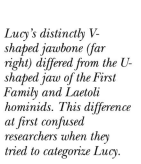
Lucy's distinctly V-shaped jawbone (far right) differed from the U-shaped jaw of the First Family and Laetoli hominids. This difference at first confused researchers when they tried to categorize Lucy.

Leakey and Johanson Agree

In 1975, Mary Leakey and Johanson met to compare the Hadar and Laetoli fossils. They agreed that Lucy was different from the First Family and the Laetoli fossils. Her teeth were smaller, and her jaw narrowed toward the front into a distinctive V shape, whereas all the other fossils had larger teeth and rounder jaws. But the main difference was body size: Lucy seemed considerably smaller. Therefore, Leakey and Johanson decided she was probably a gracile australopithecine, another dead-end branch on the ancestral bush. They also agreed that the Laetoli and First Family fossils belonged to the same group, since they had almost identical teeth and jaws. Finally, Leakey and Johanson concluded that the Laetoli and First Family fossils were the oldest early humans ever found.

After meeting with Leakey, Johanson returned to his job at the Cleveland Natural History Museum in Ohio to more closely examine his fossils. Leakey returned to her work at Laetoli. There, she hoped to find more evidence to support their theory.

Mary Leakey got what she was looking for in 1978 and 1979. At the edge of a 3.7-million-year-old volcanic ash deposit, geologist Paul Abell discovered a single hominid footprint. The footprints of two hominids were uncovered the following year. They ran side by side for 164 feet.

Although the tracks are parallel, they are less than ten inches apart, too close for the individuals to have been walking together. This led researchers to speculate that one was walking ahead of the other. One set of prints is smaller than the other, and at one point, the

Footprints found by the Leakey party in Laetoli. From the size of the prints and the length of the stride, scientists estimated one hominid was about four feet tall.

maker of those prints paused and made a half turn to the left before moving ahead again. From the size of its prints and the length of its stride, experts figure that the smaller individual was three feet, eleven inches tall. The owner of the bigger prints was about four feet, eight inches tall. The marks made by their arches, big toes, and heels are entirely like those made by modern humans.

The footprints are important for two reasons. First, they tell scientists that hominids walked upright before they developed big brains. They know this because these hominids had walked upright 700,000 years before Lucy lived, and she had a small brain of only 410cc. Second, the footprints were additional evidence that Leakey had discovered the oldest early humans. The footprints, she believed, had been made by the Laetoli hominids 3.7 million years ago.

Johanson Changes His Mind

Not everyone agreed, including Donald Johanson. By 1979, Johanson had completed his examination of Lucy and the First Family. Another paleoanthropologist, Tim White, did a similar study of the Laetoli fossils for Leakey. During their studies, the two men often conferred. Eventually, they both came to several new conclusions about the fossils.

Leakey and Johanson initially thought that Lucy was one species and the First Family and Laetoli fossils were another. Rather, all three belonged to the same species, Johanson and White decided. The differences in body, jaw, and tooth size that had led the re-

searchers to believe differently could be easily explained. In many species, females are generally smaller than males. These differences in body size and shape are called sexual dimorphism. This explained Lucy's small body and jaw size.

When White laid all the fossil jaws out on a counter in a graduated series from smallest (Lucy) to largest (one of the First Family), suddenly Lucy did not look so different. Compared to the jaws in the middle and lower end of the series, Lucy's jaw did not seem too small to be out of place.

The distinctive V shape of her jaw could also be explained. Allometry, or

The complete collection of hominid fossils from Laetoli and Hadar, neatly displayed in the lab at the Cleveland Museum of Natural History.

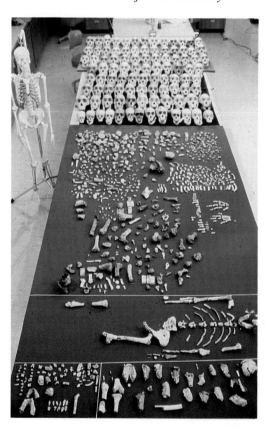

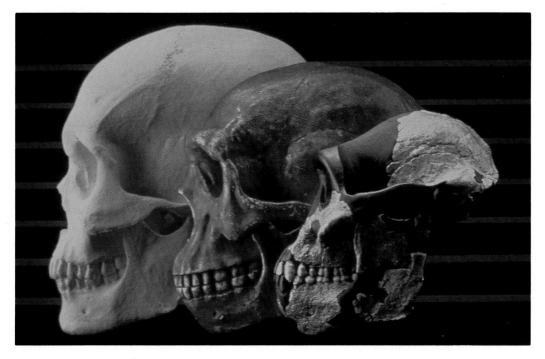

The Johanson-White theory of human origins stated that Australopithecus *(right) evolved into* Homo habilis, *which then developed into* Homo erectus *(center) which in turn became modern* Homo sapiens *(left). Comparison of the skulls clearly indicates the increase in brain size that occurred as humans evolved.*

differences in shape brought about by differences in size, was the key. Lucy's jaw was so much narrower than a male's jaw in front because her teeth were so much smaller. When White and Johanson used paper and pen to proportionally scale all the jaws down to the size of Lucy's, the differences in shape were hardly noticeable.

A New Explanation

Johanson and White did not stop there. They also concluded that Lucy, the First Family, and the Laetoli fossils belonged to a new species, one that was a common ancestor to both the australopithecines and the genus *Homo*. This species began to split into australopithecines and early humans about three million years ago, they theorized. The process probably took about one million years.

Finally, Johanson and White announced to the world that Lucy, the First Family, and the Laetoli fossils were all *Australopithecus afarensis* (southern ape from the Afar). It was the first new hominid species and the first new human ancestor to be named since Louis Leakey had named *Homo habilis*.

What Johanson and White were proposing was a new explanation of human origins. They were claiming that the ancestral ape had evolved into the oldest known human ancestor, *Australopithecus afarensis*, about four million years ago. Then three million years ago, some members of *afarensis* evolved into

An artist's depiction of Australopithecus africanus, *the gracile, or gracefully slender, hominid. A group of the apelike creatures is shown in the background chasing a hyena away from a kill.*

Australopithecus africanus, while others began the evolutionary process that would turn them into humans. That process ended about two million years ago when *afarensis* finally evolved into the first early human, *Homo habilis*. By that time, its cousin, *africanus*, had evolved into *Australopithecus robustus* and *boisei*. For the next one million years, early humans and their relatives, the robust australopithecines, lived side by side until the australopithecines became extinct. *Habilis* was the only hominid left on earth. Soon, *habilis* disappeared also. About 1.5 million years

ago, *habilis* evolved into *Homo erectus*. *Erectus*, in turn, evolved into *Homo sapiens* about 50,000 years ago.

Johanson's theory gained wide acceptance, although it did encounter some opposition. Among the dissenters are those who believe in scientific creationism. Scientific creationists do not accept evolution as part of human origins. They believe modern humans are descended from the eight people who were aboard Noah's Ark during the great biblical flood.

"There is . . . no evidence, either in the present world or in the world of the past, that Man has arisen from some 'lower' creature," says biochemist Duane Gish of the Institute for Creation Research in San Diego, California. "He stands alone as a separate and distinct created type . . . endowed with qualities that sets him far above all other living creatures."

Scientific creationists believe the australopithecines, *habilis*, and *erectus* were apes, not hominids and could not have been transitional forms between apes and modern humans. In the absence of a transitional form, creationists say, there is no fossil evidence of human evolution.

However, most scientists welcomed Johanson's interpretation of the fossils. Because his theory still maintained that an australopithecine was the oldest known human ancestor, it did not introduce too radical a change. Best of all, by finding the oldest known hominid, Johanson seemed to explain the puzzling relationship between the australopithecines and the genus *Homo*. Equally important, he had made sense of the confusing human ancestral bush.

The Knowledge Increases

By the 1970s, teams of scientists representing a wide range of knowledge and background had joined the continuing search for human origins. Some of these scientists developed new techniques to help extract additional information from fossil sites. Others spent hours in laboratories examining the fossil finds, while still others conducted laboratory studies with less traditional research materials. With the help of new technology, they found ways to extract information that otherwise would have gone unnoticed.

These scientists changed the search for human origins. It was now more than simply a quest to find hominids and untangle their relationships. Scientists were eager to know more about the hominids—how they lived, what they were like, and why they evolved as they did. New techniques and technology, combined with evidence from new fossil finds, provided volumes of new information during the 1970s and 1980s.

Closer Examination of Fossils

Lucy, for example, appears not to have been the vegetarian she was first thought to be. Closer examination of her teeth, made possible by electron microscopes that are many times more powerful than conventional microscopes, indicates that Lucy ate both meat and plants. Creatures that eat both plants and animals are called omnivores.

By examining fossil teeth using electron microscopes, anatomists learned that different types of food leave different types of scratch marks, or wear patterns, on the teeth. Vegetarians, carnivores (meat eaters), and omnivores each show a different wear pattern. So, scientists can tell what a hominid ate by identifying the wear pattern on the fossilized teeth. Magnified pictures of Lucy's teeth show the wear pattern of

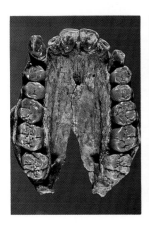
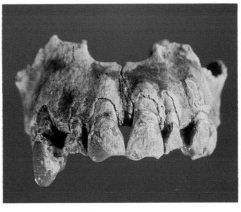

A view of Lucy's teeth from two different angles. Electron microscope studies revealed that Lucy, and presumably others of her species, ate some meat as well as plants.

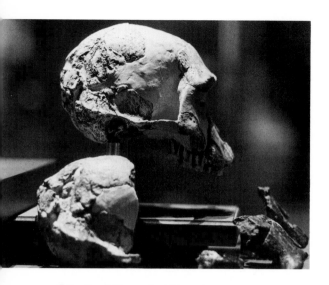

Skulls of Homo habilis, *the first early human species. Some scientists think humans made the evolutionary jump from* Australopithecus *to* Homo *as an adaptation to a dramatic change in climate and environment.*

an omnivore. This means she probably ate some meat, perhaps lizards and frogs she caught on her own or meat scavenged from kills made by predators.

Because Lucy is so old, it is difficult to learn much more about her. By studying additional *afarensis* fossils found in Africa, scientists have confirmed that the species' age is 3.7 million years old, but otherwise, they have not discovered anything significant. Work has moved forward with other fossil groups, however.

The Changing Climate

Habilis is generally accepted as the first early human. One of the most interesting questions about *habilis* is why it evolved when it did. Elisabeth Vrba, a paleontologist at Yale University, thinks she has part of the answer.

In her studies of African antelope fossils, Vrba discovered what appears to be two periods of rapid evolution interrupting the otherwise slow, steady pace of development. During these two periods, called pulses, many new antelope species appeared, and many old ones died out. The first pulse occurred about 5 million years ago, the second about 2.5 million years ago.

Geological studies indicate that the earth's climate changed during these periods from wet and warm to dry and cool. This kind of sudden and dramatic change would have forced existing species to adapt or die out. This could explain why some new antelope species appeared and others went extinct.

Two Pulses

As Vrba thought more about this, she realized that hominids might also have gone through periods of rapid evolution during the two pulses. During the

Fossil studies by Yale paleontologist Elisabeth Vrba revealed two periods of rapid evolution that may have hastened human development.

RECONSTRUCTING HUMAN ANCESTORS

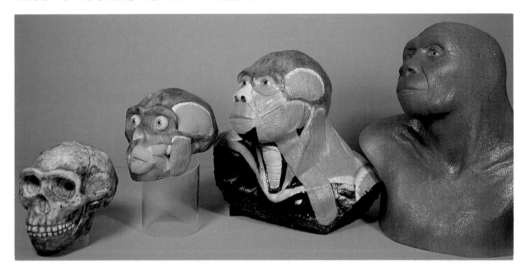

An anatomical reconstruction of a hominid.

A skeleton, even an incomplete one, tells researchers much about a human ancestor. Foot bone curves, for example, indicate whether a being walked upright; the shape of the pelvis indicates its sex. What the skeleton does not show are the vivid features of a living, breathing being. For this, scientists rely on anatomical reconstructions.

Anatomical reconstruction takes shape from the inside out, beginning with a fossil skeleton. An artist draws or builds a model of the skeleton. Grooves and marks in the bones of the skeleton tell the artist where muscles were once attached. Following these grooves and marks like a road map, the artist adds muscles to the model. The placement of the muscles, along with a detailed knowledge of ape and hominid anatomy, guides the artist in the next step: the addition of tissue and features such as eyes, nose, skin, and fur.

first pulse, about 5 million years ago, hominids probably split from apes and began evolving into australopithecines. Then, after the second pulse, 2.5 million years ago, *afarensis* disappeared and three new hominid species appeared: the two robust australopithecines, *robustus* and *boisei*, and the first member of the genus *Homo*, which was *habilis*. This, Vrba theorized, could mean that climatic changes were one of the driving forces of human origins.

Many scientists agreed with Vrba's theory. For instance, Robert Foley, an anthropologist at Cambridge University in England, feels the climatic changes that killed the forests five million years ago created the first pulse of hominid evolution. It did so by forcing many apes to come down from the disappearing trees and learn how to survive on the grasslands. Because they would then have had to forage over a greater area to find food, he says, they would have needed a more efficient means of travel. Two feet are more efficient for walking

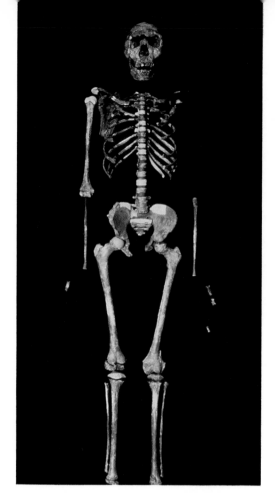

The Turkana boy skeleton is the oldest and most complete Homo erectus *ever found. It proves* erectus *originated in Africa.*

looked at *Homo*, it was randomly distributed across all the habitats. We took that to mean that *Homo* was a generalist that roamed very widely and used all kinds of resources." In other words, it seemed that *habilis* had reacted to the challenge of a changing environment by becoming an opportunist, finding and eating any kind of food any way it could. Searching through a variety of habitats for new kinds of food all the time is hard work. It requires intelligence, which promotes the development of a bigger brain.

Additional knowledge about *habilis* has come from new fossil finds in Africa. They indicate that the *habilis* brain ranged from 500 to 750cc. The creature's height ranged from 3.25 to 5.5 feet and its weight averaged 110 pounds. Scientists think *habilis* probably looked a lot like Lucy and had lots of hair. Its hands and hips, however, were more modern, and its feet were fully modern. The female members of the species were smaller than the males.

Turkana Boy

Homo habilis disappeared from the fossil record about 1.6 million years ago, at about the same time that *Homo erectus* appeared. And, like *afarensis* and *habilis*, *erectus* began in Africa, not in Java or China where it was first discovered. This was confirmed by Richard Leakey's 1.6-million-year-old fossil named Turkana boy found by Hominid Gang leader Kamoya Kimeu near Lake Turkana in 1984. It is the oldest and most complete *erectus* ever found.

Turkana boy died at age twelve. By then, he was already 5.5 feet tall. That means he could have been as tall as 6

and running than four, so gradually the apes would have become bipedal, which means walking upright on two feet.

After the second pulse, three hominid species appeared, but only *habilis* became the first early human. Foley believes he knows why *habilis* became a human ancestor and why the robust australopithecines simply went extinct. *Habilis* was the most successful mainly because it developed the biggest brain, and the reason for that bigger brain may have something to do with what it ate.

Pat Shipman of Johns Hopkins University co-led a study that analyzed fossil sites in Africa. She reported, "When we

The piece of raw rock (far left), usually obsidian, was struck along its edges with another rock to flake off chips and create a sharp edge (right). This resulted in the classic stone hand ax used by Homo erectus.

feet if he had lived to adulthood. He had a brain with a capacity in the range of 775 to 1300cc, which actually overlaps the 1000 to 2000cc range for modern humans.

Turkana boy and other new fossil finds reveal that *erectus* probably looked a great deal like *habilis*, although much bigger. Its greater intelligence is evident from its tools. *Erectus* had a wider variety of tools than *habilis*. For example, it had chisels and awls, as well as choppers and flakes. But its most unique tool is the hand ax. This fist-size tool, shaped like a flattened pear, was sharpened by striking flakes off both sides of the two long edges. This made them sharper and more versatile than the Oldowan tools of *habilis*, which had been sharpened on only one side. The hand ax is the most famous prehistoric tool. It was used for more than one million years and has been found all over Africa and Europe and in parts of India.

Modern paleoanthropologists who have become experts at making prehistoric stone tools, a process called stone knapping, have learned a great deal by using the tools. The sharp flakes apparently were used to cut the hides off animals. The hand ax was used to butcher the meat. There evidently was plenty of meat to butcher, for *erectus* left many slaughtered animal bones on its living floors. This indicates that it was a very successful hunter. It probably wandered fairly far in search of game, because some traveled at least sixty miles from the living floors to get special rock for the hand axes.

Migration Out of Africa

Many scientists think that *erectus* actually traveled a great deal farther than that. They believe sometime about one million years ago, *erectus* began to migrate out of Africa. The dating of Java man and Peking man, descendants of these migrating Africans, is still a matter of dispute. It seems likely, however, that *erectus* arrived in Java, a distance of approximately eight thousand miles by land, about 700,000 years ago. There is a great deal of disagreement over whether *erectus* lived in Europe. Numerous hand axes have been discovered there, but no undeniable *erectus* fossils have appeared.

The evidence for this migration comes from a series of *erectus* fossil sites found between Africa and China. From the dates of these sites, scientists have been able to trace parts of the migration route. The oldest site, 1.6 million years old, is in East Africa. As the route moves east toward China, the dates of the fossil sites become younger and younger.

Dating indicates that *erectus* moved into North Africa about one million years ago. Bones of slaughtered animals left on living floors in Ethiopia show *erectus* hunted hippopotamuses. Some groups settled in North Africa, but others moved on into Israel and Syria, where the same kind of evidence indicates they hunted elephants. rhinoceroses, horses, and camels. As the migration moved slowly east, some also settled in India, Russia, and Indonesia. The journey seems to have ended in China about 500,000 years ago.

Paleoanthropologists can only speculate about the reasons for this far-ranging migration. Perhaps Africa was getting crowded. Milford Wolpoff, a paleoanthropologist at the University of Michigan, said that perhaps "they left when they did because they wanted to, because they had to, and especially because they could." Perhaps they left because they were smart enough to handle the life-style changes it caused. In the colder climates north of Africa, the food supply was seasonal, making it more uncertain. *Erectus* had to learn to build shelters, make clothing, and control fire to keep out the cold.

Survival in New Habitats

Whatever the reasons for the migration, scientists think they know the results of it. Because survival in the new habitats was harder in general and demanded more intelligence, the brain of *erectus* slowly grew bigger. Then, about 500,000 years ago, the fossil record indicates something else began to happen. As its brain grew bigger, its skull became higher and rounder to accommodate the larger brain. Its face also began to change. Perhaps because *erectus* was now cooking most of its food, which made it easier to chew, its teeth became smaller. As the teeth became smaller, so did its jaws. It even began to develop a chin.

Although all members of the *erectus* species had looked similar originally, now each of the isolated populations of *erectus* began to look somewhat different. Scientists believe this is the result of living and evolving separately. For instance, the *erectus* in North Africa had no contact with those in India, and the *erectus* in Israel had no contact with those in China. But, even with their differences, all the evolving *erectus* populations were beginning to look much like modern humans, *Homo sapiens*, with a combination of *erectus* and *sapiens* characteristics.

Multiregional Theory

Most paleoanthropologists believe these various changes in the *erectus* populations are signs that they were evolving into modern humans. Currently, the most widely accepted theory on the origin of modern humans, called the multiregional theory, claims that after *erectus* migrated out of Africa one million years ago, it evolved into modern humans in many areas of the world simultaneously. The *erectus* in China evolved into the modern Chinese, the *erectus* in Africa

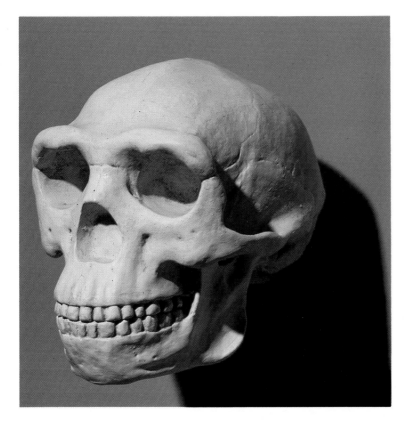

Skull of Peking man, a type of Homo erectus. Erectus *disappears from the fossil record about 200,000 years ago.*

evolved into the modern Africans, and so on. Because these populations evolved separately, they evolved into different races. That is why the human races—for example, Mongoloid, Caucasian, and Negroid—all look somewhat different. But, according to this theory, they are all the same species and look basically alike because of interbreeding among all the populations.

Erectus disappeared from the fossil record about 200,000 years ago, but no modern human fossils that old have been found. All the fossils that age have a blend of *erectus* and modern characteristics. Because of this, scientists believe each population of *erectus* either evolved into a transitional form between *erectus* and modern humans or went extinct.

These transitional forms are now all called *Homo sapiens*, or archaic humans (archaics). Before the archaics were identified, the name *Homo sapiens* belonged to modern humans. After they were identified, the Latin name for modern humans was changed to *Homo sapiens sapiens* to differentiate them from the archaics.

On the whole, archaics are a mysterious group. They are lumped together in the transitional period between two species. Because each population is somewhat different, there is no simple way to define them and no easy way to identify them. Also, scientists have the same problem with them that they do with all transitional forms: for a long period in the fossil record, it is almost impossible for scientists to tell whether a fossil is still *erectus* or has crossed the line and become an archaic. It is equally dif-

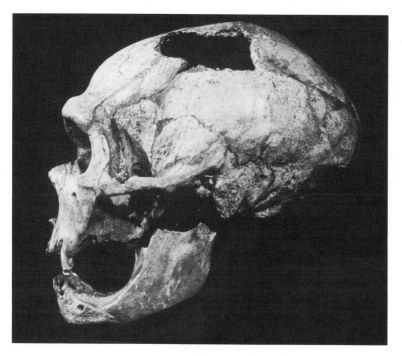

A Neandertal skull. Scientists are undecided about where Neandertals fit in the human origins puzzle. Some experts think Neandertals interbred with their human neighbors. Others believe they simply died out.

ficult to tell when an archaic has crossed the line and become fully modern. In fact, says Milford Wolpoff, "the closer you look, the messier it gets."

The majority of paleoanthropologists believe that most populations of archaics evolved into modern humans, but some of them do note one famous exception. That exception is Neandertal man, who is now considered an archaic. Neandertal man's Latin name is *Homo sapiens neanderthalensis.*

Many scientists still believe the Neandertals went extinct without evolving into modern humans. They have no other way to explain why they apparently lived side by side with modern humans for so long. But, by the mid 1980s, some paleoanthropologists had begun to believe the Neandertals were human ancestors in another sense.

Since the Neandertals lived alongside modern humans and other archaics in many of the same areas, these scientists think some interbreeding probably occurred. If this is so, modern humans carry some Neandertal genes, which makes Neandertal man a human ancestor after all.

In 1987, scientists who believed the Neandertals might be human ancestors were beginning to gather evidence to prove it. Then, unexpectedly, a new theory about the origin of modern humans was announced. According to this new theory, the Neandertals are definitely not human ancestors. This put Neandertal man right in the middle of the controversy over the most unusual discovery paleoanthropology had ever seen. After this discovery, the search for human origins would never be the same.

The Mother of Us All

On January 1, 1987, three scientists from the University of California at Berkeley made an astonishing announcement. Rebecca Cann, Mark Stoneking, and Allan Wilson claimed they had found the oldest common ancestor of all modern humans. This ancestor was a female who lived in Africa about 200,000 years ago. The three scientists called her the "mother of us all." Soon, others were calling her Eve.

The Eve Theory

The Eve theory represented a huge departure from standard thinking about human origins. First, the theory was developed after a discovery was made in a laboratory rather than in the field. Not a single fossil contributed to the theory.

Second, the Eve theory contradicted the most widely accepted theory of human origins, which was the multi-regional theory. The accepted theory claimed that several *erectus* populations simultaneously evolved into modern humans (through transitional archaics) in different parts of the world and that this evolution began a million years ago when these populations left Africa. The Eve theory, on the other hand, suggested that one group of archaics located in Africa gave rise to all modern humans and that the process began about 200,000 years ago.

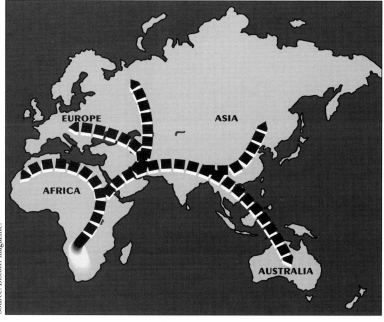

Source: *Discover* magazine.

According to the Eve theory, all modern humans are descended from one African woman. Her descendants migrated to other regions of the world, as indicated by the arrows, and became the ancestors of all humans on earth today.

Scientist Rebecca Cann from the University of California at Berkeley co-authored the Eve theory of human evolution, which is based on DNA studies rather than fossil evidence.

Finally, when the descendants of those archaics migrated out of Africa, they completely replaced all other *erectus* and archaic populations, according to the Eve theory. Not a single member of those other groups survived, and no instances of interbreeding occurred. This meant that those groups were not ancestors of modern humans. In other words, all modern humans are descended from one group of archaics who lived in Africa about 200,000 years ago.

Most paleoanthropologists rejected the Eve study completely. They agreed with paleoanthropologist Phillip Tobias when he said, "I can't really find any biological feasibility in the suggestion of one small single group arising in Africa and pushing out—totally supersed-

ing—all of mankind in Europe . . . in Asia . . . in Australia and everywhere else."

Other scientists, however, including Mary Leakey, saw potential in this new study. "I think people have gotten over-enthusiastic," she said, "and they are probably claiming more than they can at the moment. But once it stabilizes I think it can be extremely significant."

The DNA Link

The Berkeley scientists who proposed the Eve theory developed it through research on a substance from the human body called mitochondrial deoxyribonucleic acid (mtDNA). Mitochondria are long, thin strips of proteins that float around in human cells. Cells are the microscopic building blocks of all living organisms, and they require energy to perform the various tasks that keep an organism alive. Mitochondria turn chemicals into the energy needed by the cells. Also, mitochondria contain a small amount of DNA.

DNA contains the genes that direct which characteristics will pass from parents to offspring. Most DNA is found in the center, or nucleus, of cells and is passed to offspring from both male and female parents.

Mitochondrial DNA, however, passes to offspring in a different way. It is this difference that intrigued the Berkeley scientists. The mtDNA is transmitted to offspring only from the mother's egg, not from the father's sperm. This means that mtDNA is not a scrambled mixture of the mother's and father's genes. So, every female's mtDNA contains a pure maternal ancestral tree. This tree enables scientists to

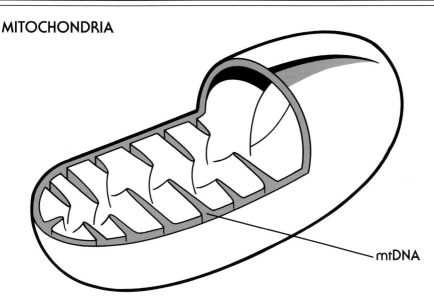

MITOCHONDRIA

mtDNA

Five billion years ago, a small, air-breathing bacterium is thought to have worked its way inside the walls of a primitive cell. The bacterium became trapped, but did not die. It found a ready source of food inside the cells. As the bacteria broke down this food, they released a great deal of chemical energy. This energy was very useful to the host cells. A mutually beneficial, or symbiotic, relationship developed between the bacteria and the cells. The bacteria became a permanent part of the cell, known as mitochondria.

Mitochondria continue to break down food and provide life-giving energy to the body's cells. They also hold a small amount of DNA, a substance that contains the information that determines each person's physical makeup. Mitochondrial DNA (mtDNA) is different from the DNA found elsewhere in the body in at least one respect: it is transmitted to offspring only in the mother's egg, not in the father's sperm. This means mtDNA is passed to offspring unscrambled by the merging of egg and sperm. With sophisticated laboratory tests the intact mtDNA from different groups of people can be compared and traced back to their common ancestors. Researchers used this technique to identify the mitochondrial Eve.

look back into the female past, in a straight line from daughter to mother to grandmother, and so on.

Mutations

Usually, mtDNA passes from mother to daughter unchanged. Sometimes, however, it does change. This happens during mitochondrial reproduction. To reproduce, mitochondria first manufacture an exact copy of their mtDNA. Then, the mitochondria split in half, creating two copies of each original mitochondrion. Each new mitochondrion contains a duplicate copy of the mtDNA. Occasionally, however, a mistake is made during this copying process, and the new mtDNA contains a small error called a mutation.

Mutations accumulate over time because each one is passed down to all the following generations of females through the mtDNA in the mother's egg. Every time a new mutation is added to the ones already accumulated, it creates a different pattern in the mtDNA. Since each pattern is unique, scientists can identify and count them to determine how many mutations have occurred.

The Molecular Clock

Although mtDNA mutates only occasionally, some scientists believe these mutations occur at a fixed, constant rate. They think this rate is as regular as a clock and therefore refer to it as the molecular clock.

If this theory is correct, then a scientist should be able to use a mathematical formula to calculate the frequency of mutations going back millions of years. This is precisely what the Berkeley scientists did. They calculated that mutations accumulate in the mtDNA at a fixed rate of 2 to 4 percent every one million years. Using a mathematical formula, they could then figure out how long it would take for all the mutations they counted to occur. That would tell them when the mtDNA first appeared.

With an understanding of mtDNA and the molecular clock, the Berkeley biochemists decided to compare the mtDNA of the various modern human races to find out how they differed. Then, by using the molecular clock, they could calculate how long it took for those differences to accumulate. In theory, this information would accomplish three things.

First, by tracing mtDNA mutations back to their earliest appearance, the biochemists would find the oldest race of modern humans. Second, by determining the geographical location of the oldest race, the scientists would discover the birthplace of modern humans. Third, by using the molecular clock to

Mark Stoneking was one of the three Berkeley scientists whose genetics research led to the formulation of the Eve theory.

determine when the oldest common ancestor lived, they would know the birth date of modern humans.

The Eve Study

To test their theory, the three Berkeley scientists began a study in 1985. They tested the mtDNA of 147 women of different races. A second study was done in 1991 with a different group of 189 women representing different races. Both studies led to the same conclusion: all modern humans share a common ancestor who lived in Africa about 200,000 years ago, and that ancestor is represented by a symbolic Eve.

Cann, Stoneking, and Wilson were proud of their theory. They thought it had not only contributed new knowledge to the search for human origins but had broken new ground by using a unique approach to the search. This approach depended on the techniques of molecular biology, the science of using genetic information to explain biological phenomena, such as human origins. Molecular biology studies do not require the discovery of a rare new hominid fossil. The materials they require exist in every modern human. And these studies can provide information that fossils will never be able to provide.

Wilson said, "The molecules of life are now the chief source of new insights into the nature of the evolutionary process." A few paleoanthropologists agreed with him. They also felt that scientists would come to depend on molecular biology studies in the future, and they were excited about the Eve theory.

One of these scientists, Stephen Jay Gould, a paleontologist at Harvard Uni-

The late Allan Wilson, a Berkeley professor of cell biology, helped develop the Eve theory, along with Cann and Stoneking.

versity, is quoted in *Newsweek* as saying:

> If it's correct, and I'd put money on it, this idea is tremendously important. It makes us realize that all human beings, despite differences in external appearance, are really members of a single entity that's had a very recent origin in one place. There is a kind of biological brotherhood that's much more profound than we ever realized.

Some other paleoanthropologists welcomed the Eve theory because they believed it substantiated their own beliefs. Years before the Eve theory was introduced, they postulated that modern humans evolved just once in one place and considered Africa the most likely spot. According to this theory, modern humans all looked alike in the beginning. Then, after they migrated out of Africa and settled in separate groups all over Asia and Europe, each group evolved into a different race as it adapted to its new environment. Both this theory and the Eve theory are now often referred to as the out-of-Africa theory.

Most Scientists Disagree

Most paleoanthropologists, however, rejected the Eve study completely. "Wacko" was Milford Wolpoff's response. Wolpoff is perhaps the theory's most vocal opponent, and he summarizes his case against it by citing two points. First, Wolpoff disputes the concept of a regular molecular clock. Unseen and unknowable factors make it impossible for scientists to accurately count mtDNA mutations, Wolpoff says, and without an accurate count any molecular clock would be flawed. Because of this, Wolpoff believes, the Eve theorists miscalculated the time of the hominid migration out of Africa.

The gap between the multiregional theory, which Wolpoff supports, and the Eve theory, grew even wider in 1992. New information presented at a

University of Michigan paleoanthropologist Milford Wolpoff is the Eve theory's most vocal critic. He calls the theory "wacko" and prefers the multiregional theory.

meeting of the American Association for the Advancement of Science added further support to the multiregional theory and raised new doubts about Eve.

This information concerned Neandertal man. Many scientists had believed that Neandertal man was an archaic species that died out without contributing anything to human ancestry.

In February 1992, however, Wolpoff announced new evidence suggesting that Neandertal man is actually an ancestor of modern Europeans. Scientists had already found a number of Neandertal characteristics in modern Europeans. If true, this finding would bolster the multiregional theory and refute the Eve theory.

The evidence came from several different sources. University of Pennsylvania anthropologist Alan Mann compared teeth from the Neandertals, modern Europeans, and Africans. Under the electron microscope, he found differences in the enamel of teeth from Europeans and Africans. However, the enamel of European and Neandertal teeth was the same. "If the African Eve is correct," Mann said, "then the Europeans should share their tooth structures with Africans. That is not the case."

Two other anthropologists, Rachel Caspari of Albion College in Michigan and David Frayer of the University of Kansas at Lawrence, conducted new studies on skull anatomy. They found that the temporal area (the area near the temple) of the Neandertal skulls got smaller and thinner over time. As this happened, the temporal areas increasingly resembled those of modern Europeans. Caspari said these similarities indicate "a continuity in defining charac-

teristics" that show Neandertals could be human ancestors. Also, Neandertal brain casts by Ralph Holloway revealed that Neandertal brains have the same structure overall as those of modern humans.

Another Dispute

Because this evidence is so new, it is still controversial. Although many scientists think it is evidence worth considering, those who believe in the out-of-Africa theory are not convinced. Paleoanthropologist Christopher Stringer at the Natural History Museum in London is one of those who doubt the new evidence. Stringer has been one of the strongest supporters of the out-of-Africa theory, and he still believes what he said in *Newsweek* in 1988:

> I don't rule out the possibility that there was interbreeding, but I don't see it in the fossils. In the two areas [where] we have the best fossil evidence, Europe and Southwest Asia, the gap between archaic and modern people is very large. The entire skeleton and brain case changed. I think the fossil evidence is clearly signaling replacement of the archaic population. I was delighted to see the DNA results support this view.

More Controversy

However, research made public in 1992 raised more doubt about both the Eve and out-of-Africa theories. A team of scientists from Harvard University, Washington University, and Pennsylvania State University reanalyzed data from the 1987 Eve study and found two contradictions. First, the researchers said,

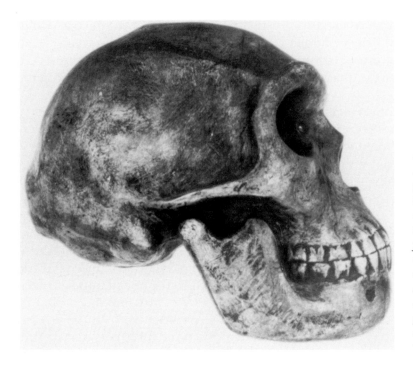

Side view of a Neandertal skull. A gradual shrinking and thinning of the temporal bone (behind the eye ridge and above the jaw) of Neandertals eventually gave them a look similar to modern Europeans. Some scientists believe this is proof that Neandertals could be ancestors of modern humans.

the Berkeley scientists had based their theory on a flawed computer analysis. Second, the new study indicated that Eve could have come from either Africa or Asia.

This conclusion took on even greater significance in June 1992. In an article in the British journal, *Nature*, Chinese and American researchers announced they had uncovered evidence indicating that modern humans evolved at the same time in both Africa and Asia.

Researchers Li Tianyun of the Hubei Institute of Archeology in China and Dennis A. Etler of the University of California at Berkeley based their conclusion on analysis of two skulls found near China's Han River in 1989 and 1990. The 350,000-year-old skulls have a mix of *erectus* and archaic features as well as some distinctly Chinese features. The backs of the skulls are sharp and angular like most *erectus* skulls. The faces are broad and flat and the cheekbones high like most archaic skulls. The faces and teeth, however, have features found only among the Chinese population.

Taken together, the researchers said, these characteristics indicate that modern humans may have their origins in more than one place. "We think these finds . . . suggest that certain features of the modern anatomy were reached in Asia," Etler told the *Los Angeles Times*. "There is no indication of a replacement of the more ancient Asians by more modern people from another part of the world."

The Future

Studies based on mtDNA ushered in a new age for paleoanthropology, but they are only the beginning of the change molecular biology will make in the search for human origins. When the studies are based on nuclear DNA—the DNA found in the cell nuclei instead of mtDNA—many more scientists will believe their results.

The genes in DNA are passed down from both parents to their offspring. These genes determine all the physical characteristics of individuals, from body shape to eye color. Because of this, DNA has a far greater influence on human evolution than mtDNA. That means the results of studies using DNA will carry greater weight. But DNA is very complicated. No one yet understands it well enough to use it in such studies.

Fortunately, the day is coming when that will change. The U.S. government has funded a three-billion-dollar project to decipher and map all the genes in human DNA. This incredibly difficult task, expected to take fifteen years, should be completed by about the year 2000. At that time, it might be possible to confirm the mtDNA studies as well as discover many other things about human origins. Already, this branch of molecular biology is being called molecular anthropology. These new specialists feel the information they can gather from DNA studies is virtually endless.

A map of the DNA of one human chromosome. Future DNA studies will surely provide some answers to questions about human origins.

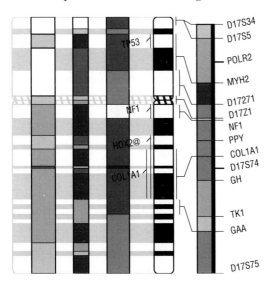

Sources of Ancient DNA

For example, scientists hope that extracting DNA from long-extinct hominid species will provide answers to questions about human kinships, ancient migrations, and rates of evolution. They first have to learn, however, how to do the extractions correctly.

In some of the first experiments of this type, scientists have successfully extracted DNA from a twenty-four-hundred-year-old Egyptian mummy and from seventy-five-hundred-year-old human brain cells. Someday, it might be possible to find DNA in Neandertal, *habilis,* or *erectus* fossils. Their DNA would allow scientists to determine once and for all whether they are human ancestors. They would do this by extracting the genes from their DNA and determining whether any of those genes are found in modern humans.

Canadian scientist Thomas Loy has discovered another possible source of ancient DNA that could help solve the mystery of human origins. He found blood cells on some ancient stone tools, including tools from Iraq that he believes may be Neandertal. If any of the blood is human, it will provide molecular anthropologists with a perfect research material. Loy states:

> We're sitting on a land mine of knowledge. Within the next five years, we'll be able to recover blood residues from stone tools over the entire course of human history. If we have blood from a Neandertal and blood from Lucy, we can determine the point that we crossed the threshold into being us and trace the entire lineage of humankind.

More Fossils to Be Discovered

However, the future of paleoanthropology does not lie completely in the laboratory. Paleoanthropologists will continue to pursue the search for fossils because bones are still the most important concrete evidence of human origins.

It is doubtful that search will ever be concluded. Some experts estimate that more than five billion hominids lived between five million years ago when they first appeared and ten thousand years ago. Only about 2,500 of them, or 1 out of every 200 million, have been found, most of them since 1920.

In all probability, the few hominids that have been found are only a small fraction of all the different types of hominids that lived during that period. This means current knowledge about human ancestry is only a small portion of the truth. Future fossil finds will surely increase that knowledge.

Fossil finds will probably increase in the future because new technology will make it easier to find fossil sites. It is already no longer necessary to spend years trying to find potentially good sites. Satellites orbiting the earth provide detailed pictures of the earth's surface, which help to pinpoint promising sites.

In 1990, a team of paleoanthropologists used satellite images to find potentially rich fossil beds in the Fejej region of Ethiopia. When they climbed to the

Human brain cells. By extracting DNA from human brain cells, scientists hope to learn more about human evolution.

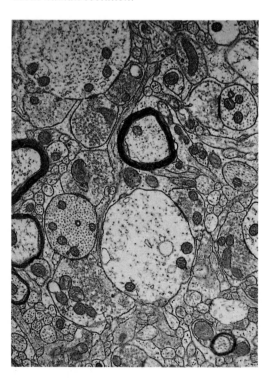

top of one bluff they had identified from a satellite photograph, they found 3.7-million-year-old fossil teeth from *Australopithecus afarensis*.

In the future, satellite images will be so sharp they may actually show paleoanthropologists the insides of certain deposits. Satellites are already capable of mapping underground water systems. Since fossils are often found near rivers and lakes, these maps will be very helpful when they become available.

Using Radar

Some of the new techniques paleoanthropologists will be using in the future sound like science fiction, but they are very real possibilities. One technique is called ground-penetrating radar. This is a microwave radar that can "see" underground. Microwaves are beamed into the ground, and the waves bounce off, or echo off, buried objects. By measuring the length of the echoes on a radar screen, scientists can map the position of objects in an underground area.

Some experts believe this technology will eventually become so advanced that scientists will be able to see buried fossils in clear detail on a computer screen. Paleoanthropologist Tim White is somewhat more skeptical: "You're

Satellite technology is becoming an important archaeological tool. Using satellite pictures, fossil hunters in Ethiopia found a bluff where 3.7-million-year-old fossil teeth were found.

never going to be able to sit in the lab and say, 'There's a skeleton.'"

Taking core samples is another technique that will soon make fossils easier to find. Satellite images can tell scientists the best places to take these samples. To take a core sample, a scien-

This satellite photo of a mountainous region of Peru was taken by the space shuttle Challenger. *Such photos can help scientists determine the location of fossil beds.*

A woodcut of Neandertal cave dwellers. Continuing studies and new technology will slowly replace fanciful depictions of human ancestors with factual ones.

tist drills straight down deep into the earth with a round, hollow drill and brings up a cylinder of earth, or core, with all the layers or deposits still in place. Paleoanthropologists can then determine what deposit, if any, is most likely to contain fossils and where exactly that deposit lies.

The best thing about these new technologies is that they will greatly increase the number of places where paleoanthropologists can look for fossils. Up until now, scientists have found their fossils either in caves or lying exposed on the ground. They have seldom dug underground to find fossils because they had no way of knowing where to dig. There must be many fossils lying hidden under layers of rock, and soon paleoanthropologists will have a way to find them.

The Future Focus

The focus of paleoanthropology will likely change in the future, too. Current knowledge indicates that human origins are extremely complicated. If the Eve theory is correct, the human ancestral bush has side branches shooting out all over the place. Among them are all the separate populations of *erectus* and archaics outside Africa. They are now the most fascinating mystery in paleoanthropology. They all had the potential of becoming human. Now, it seems possible that only one succeeded.

No one really understands why some hominids became human ancestors and others went extinct. Many hominids existed side by side, competing for survival, and extinction was a common occurrence. To understand the human species, we need to know why our ancestors were the ones to survive. We cannot do that without understanding why the other hominids went extinct.

As a result, the focus on finding the oldest hominid will likely be replaced by an emphasis on finding the youngest hominids. In other words, paleoanthropologists will look for the last surviving individual of all the extinct hominids, including the robust australopithecines, Java man, Peking man, and Neandertal man. They will look for explanations of why these hominids failed to adapt to the conditions that existed while they were evolving. To do that, they will have to understand the ecosystem in which those hominids evolved. An ecosystem refers to the interrelationships among all parts of a particular environment, including all the natural events that occur there and all the creatures that live in it.

Paleoanthropology studies alone cannot provide this understanding. In the future, paleoanthropology may become part of a new, broader science called, perhaps, evolutionary ecology. These scientists might study not only human origins but also humanity's place in nature. More and more, scientists have come to believe that humans are not the inevitable end product of evolution. Given the many possible paths evolution can take, they find it amazing that we are here at all. It may be the job of evolutionary ecologists— or other scientists of the future—to find out why.

Glossary

■■■

anthropology: The scientific study of human origins, cultures, and biological characteristics.

archaeology: The scientific study of ancient peoples and their cultures through analysis of tools, art, and other remains of their lives.

archaics: The human ancestors who lived between 500,000 and 100,000 years ago and evolved from *Homo erectus* into modern humans.

australopithecine: A hominid that is a member of the genus *Australopithecus*.

Australopithecus afarensis: The Latin name means "southern ape from the Afar" and refers to Lucy, the oldest known human ancestor.

Australopithecus africanus: The Latin name means "southern ape from Africa" and refers to a hominid descended from *Australopithecus afarensis* that is not a human ancestor.

Australopithecus boisei: The Latin name means "Boise's southern ape" and refers to Zinj, a hominid descended from *Australopithecus africanus* that is not a human ancestor.

Australopithecus robustus: The Latin name means "robust southern ape" and refers to a hominid descended from *Australopithecus africanus* that is not a human ancestor.

bipedal: Having two feet and walking upright.

carnivore: An animal that eats primarily meat.

comparative anatomy: The scientific study of the differences and similarities between the structure of humans and all related species.

DNA: Deoxyribonucleic acid; a substance that contains the genes that direct which characteristics will pass from parents to offspring.

evolution: The process of gradual change from one type of life-form to another by means of mutations in the genes.

fluorine dating: A method of determing the relative age of a fossil by measuring the amount of fluorine gas found in the fossil.

fossil: The remains of a plant or animal preserved in rock.

gene: The basic unit of heredity contained in DNA that determines every physical characteristic of every living thing.

gracile: Gracefully slender; refers to *Australopithecus africanus* and *afarensis*.

hominid: Any primate who is an ancestor of or is related to humans.

Homo erectus: The Latin name means "upright man" and refers to a human ancestor who lived from 1.6 million years ago to 200,000 years ago; *erectus* evolved into *Homo sapiens*.

Homo sapiens: The Latin name means "wise man" and refers to the human ancestors who lived from 500,000 to

100,000 years ago and evolved from *erectus* into modern humans; also known as the archaics.

Homo sapiens neanderthalensis: The Latin name means "wise man from the Neander Valley" and refers to an archaic who lived between 125,000 and 30,000 years ago.

Homo sapiens sapiens: The Latin name means "doubly wise man" and refers to modern humans who evolved about 100,000 years ago.

living floor: A site where prehistoric hominids camped to slaughter animals for food and perhaps to sleep.

mitochondria: Long, thin strips of proteins that float in the cells; they turn chemicals into the energy needed by the cells.

mitochondrial deoxyribonucleic acid (mtDNA): The DNA contained in mitochondria; it is found only in female egg cells.

molecular anthropology: The scientific study of human origins in the laboratory using DNA as the primary research material.

mutations: Any mistake that occurs when the DNA splits to form a copy of itself during cell reproduction.

omnivore: An animal that eats both plants and other animals.

paleoanthropology: The scientific study of human fossils to determine human origins.

paleontology: The scientific study of fossils.

Pithecanthropus erectus: The Latin name for Java man, identified by its discoverer as the missing link; the name was later changed to *Homo erectus.*

primate: A biologically similar group of mammals that includes humans, apes, monkeys, and related species.

sexual dimorphism: The existence of two different forms within a species so that the males and females look different in regard to size, color, or form.

Sinanthropus pekinensis: The first Latin name given to Peking man; the name was later changed to *Homo erectus.*

tuff: A volcanic deposit.

Zinjanthropus boisei (Zinj): The first Latin name for *Australopithecus boisei.*

For Further Reading

■■

Jean-Jacques Barloy, *Prehistory: From Australopithecus to Mammoth Hunters.* New York: Barron's Educational Series, 1987.

Joanna Cole, *The Human Body: How We Evolved.* New York: William Morrow, 1987.

Bruce Coville, *Prehistoric People.* New York: Doubleday, 1990.

Dougal Dixon, *After Man: A Zoology of the Future.* New York: St. Martin's Press, 1981.

Roy A. Gallant, *Before the Sun Dies: The Story of Evolution.* New York: Macmillan, 1989.

F. Clark Howell, *Early Man.* New York: Time-Life Books, 1968. Revised, 1977.

David Lambert and the Diagram Group, *The Field Guide to Early Man.* New York: Facts on File, 1987.

Christopher Lampton, *New Theories on the Origins of the Human Race.* New York: Franklin Watts, 1989.

Kathryn Lasky, *Traces of Life: The Origins of Humankind.* New York: Morrow Junior Books, 1989.

Richard E. Leakey, *Human Origins.* New York: Lodestar Books, 1982.

Let's Discover the Prehistoric World. Milwaukee, WI: Raintree, 1979.

Tom McGowen, *Album of Prehistoric Man.* New York: Checkerboard Press, 1987.

Henri de Saint-Blanquat, *The First People.* Morristown, NJ: Silver Burdett, 1986.

Helen Roney Sattler, *Hominids: A Look Back at Our Ancestors.* New York: Lothrop, Lee & Shepard, 1988.

John Stidworthy, *When Humans Began.* Morristown, NJ: Silver Burdett, 1986.

Works Consulted

■■

William F. Allman, "The First Humans," *U.S. News & World Report*, February 27, 1989.

William F. Allman, "Who We Were," *U.S. News & World Report*, September 16, 1991.

Peter J. Bowler, *Charles Darwin: The Man and His Influence*. Cambridge, MA: Basil Blackwell, 1990.

Michael H. Brown, *The Search for Eve*. New York: HarperCollins, 1990.

Jeremy Cherfas, "Ancient DNA: Still Busy After Death," *Science*, September 20, 1991.

Joshua Fischman, "Hard Evidence," *Discover*, February 1992.

Robert A. Foley, "The Search for Early Man," *Archaeology*, January/February 1989.

Ann Gibbons, "A 'New Look' for Archeology," *Science*, May 17, 1991.

Duane T. Gish, *Evolution: The Challenge of the Fossil Record*. El Cajon, CA: Creation-Life, 1985.

Donald Johanson and James Shrieve, *Lucy's Child: The Discovery of a Human Ancestor*. New York: William Morrow, 1989.

Donald Johanson and Maitland Edey, *Lucy: The Beginnings of Humankind*. New York: Simon & Schuster, 1981.

Richard E. Leakey, *The Making of Mankind*. New York: E. P. Dutton, 1981.

Richard E. Leakey and Roger Lewin, *Origins*. New York: E. P. Dutton, 1977.

Richard E. Leakey and Roger Lewin, *People of the Lake: Mankind and Its Beginnings*. Garden City, NY: Anchor Press/Doubleday, 1978.

Roger Lewin, *Bones of Contention: Controversies in the Search for Human Origins*. New York: Simon & Schuster, 1987.

Roger Lewin, "Conflict over DNA Clock Results,"

Science, September 23, 1988.

Roger Lewin, "The Unmasking of Mitochondrial Eve," *Science*, October 2, 1987.

C. Owen Lovejoy, "Evolution of Human Walking," *Scientific American*, November 1988.

Linda Marsa, "Family Tree: Blood Samples from Prehistoric Stone Tools May Help Identify Our Ancestry," *Omni*, November 1990.

Thomas H. Maught II, "Study Boosts Neanderthal into Human Family Tree," *Los Angeles Times*, February 9, 1992.

Neil McAleer, "Pixel Archeology," *Discover*, August 1988.

National Science Foundation Mosaic Reader: Human Evolution. Wayne, NJ: Avery Publishing Group, 1983.

John Reader, *Missing Links: The Hunt for Earliest Man.* Boston: Little, Brown, 1981.

Harry L. Shapiro, *Peking Man.* New York: Simon & Schuster, 1974.

Pat Shipman, "An Age-Old Problem: Why Did the Human Lineage Survive?" *Discover*, April 1987.

James Shreeve, "Argument over a Woman," *Discover*, August 1990.

William K. Stevens, "Global Climate Changes Seen as Force in Human Evolution," *The New York Times*, October 16, 1990.

John Tierney, Lynda Wright, and Karen Springen, "The Search for Adam and Eve," *Newsweek*, January 11, 1988.

Linda Vigilant, Mark Stoneking, Henry Harpending, Kristen Hawkes and Allan C. Wilson, "African Populations and the Evolution of Human Mitochondrial DNA," *Science*, September 27, 1991.

Kenneth F. Weaver, "The Search for Our Ancestors," *National Geographic*, November 1985.

Herbert Wendt, *From Ape to Adam.* New York: Bobbs-Merrill, 1972.

John Noble Wilford, "Fossil Findings Fan Debate on Human Origins," *The New York Times*, February 14, 1989.

John Noble Wilford, "Teeth Carry Clues to Diet of the Extinct," *The New York Times*, October 16, 1990.

John Noble Wilford, "2.4-Million-Year Link to Man Found," *San Diego Union-Tribune*, February 20, 1992.

Index

About the Author

Lois Warburton earned her master's degree in education at Clark University in Worcester, Massachusetts. Her previous published works include nonfiction articles, magazine columns, short stories, and poetry. In 1990, she retired from her own word processing, writing, and editing business to travel and write books. Warburton has written six books for Lucent Books.

Picture Credits

Cover photo: FPG International. American Museum of Natural History, 16 (bottom), neg. no. 319712; 16 (top), neg. no. 318607; 25, neg. no. 27935, J. Kirschner; 29, neg. no. 298897; 31, neg. no. 319781; 32, neg. no. 323737, ROTA; 33 (top), neg. no. 123868; 33 (bottom), neg. no. 327937, J. Leon Williams; 34, neg. no. 315450; 35, neg. no. 315447, C. H. Coles; 36, neg. no. 335653; 38, neg. no. 109353; 39, neg. no. 123869; 46, neg. no. 33509, Singer; 69, neg. no. 335039, Singer. AP/ Wide World, 20. Archiv des Ernst-Haeckel-Hauses, Friedrich-Schiller-Universität Jena, 26 (bottom), 27. The Bettmann Archive, 12, 14 (right), 44 (bottom), 84. Robert Caldwell, 17, 22, 30, 55, 75. Field Museum of Natural History, (Neg. #76851), Chicago, 37. The Granger Collection, 13. Historical Pictures, 15. Ralph Holloway, Columbia University, 54 (bottom). George Holton, Photo Researchers, 52 (top). Institute of Human Origins, 40, 48, 57, 58, 61 (top, right), 62, 63, 65 (both). Bob Kalmbach, 78. Ed Kashi, *Discover* magazine, 76. Library of Congress, 19. © Tom McHugh, Photo Researchers, 71. Bill Munns, 60. Bill Munns/San Diego Museum of Man, 67. Musée de l'Homme, Paris, 42, 72. National Aeronautics and Space Administration, 83 (bottom). National Library of Medicine, 26 (top), 28. The National Museums of Kenya, 49, 50 (both), 51, 52 (bottom), 53 (both), 54 (top), 61 (top, left), 61 (bottom), 68. The Natural History Museum, London, 18, 64. Courtesy of the George C. Page Museum, 14 (left). © Bill Pierce, Rainbow, 82. From *Prehistoric Man* by Bratislav Mazak, illustrated by Zdenek Burian. New York: The Hamlyn Publishing Group, 1980, 41. John Reader/Science Photo Library, 43, 56 (both), 59. San Diego Museum of Man, 80. Jane Scherr, 77. *Science* magazine, 81. Seth Shostak/Science Photo Library, 83 (top). University of Illinois Library at Urbana-Champaign, 23. Courtesy University of Minnesota Libraries, 24. UPI/Bettmann, 44 (top), 45, 47, 66 (top). Elisabeth Vrba, 66 (bottom). James D. Wilson, *Newsweek*, 74.